# HAIL, CAESAR!

# HAIL, CAESAR!

*Joel Coen and Ethan Coen*

FABER & FABER

First published in 2016
by Faber & Faber Limited
Bloomsbury House
74–77 Great Russell Street
London WC1B 3DA

Typeset by Country Setting, Kingsdown, Kent CT14 8ES
Printed in the UK by CPI Group (UK) Ltd, Croydon CR0 4YY

A CIP record for this book
is available from the British Library

ISBN 978-0-571-33122-2

2 4 6 8 10 9 7 5 3 1

# Cast and Crew

*Hail, Caesar!* was first shown
at the Berlin Film Festival on 11 February 2016

### PRINCIPAL CAST

| | |
|---|---|
| EDDIE MANNIX | Josh Brolin |
| BAIRD WHITLOCK | George Clooney |
| HOBIE DOYLE | Alden Ehrenreich |
| LAURENCE LAURENTZ | Ralph Fiennes |
| DEEANNA MORAN | Scarlett Johansson |
| THORA THACKER | Tilda Swinton |
| BURT GURNEY | Channing Tatum |
| C. C. CALHOUN | Frances McDormand |
| JOE SILVERMAN | Jonah Hill |
| CARLOTTA VALDEZ | Veronica Osorio |
| THESSALY THACKER | Tilda Swinton |
| NATALIE | Heather Goldenhersh |
| MRS MANNIX | Alison Pill |
| JOHN HOWARD HERMAN | Max Baker |
| PROFESSOR MARCUSE | John Bluthal |

### PRINCIPAL CREW

| | |
|---|---|
| *Written and Directed by* | Joel Coen and Ethan Coen |
| *Produced by* | Tim Bevan |
| | Eric Fellner |
| | Joel Coen |
| | Ethan Coen |
| | Ralph Graf |
| *Cinematography by* | Roger Deakins |
| *Editing by* | Roderick Jaynes |
| *Music by* | Carter Burwell |
| *Production Design by* | Jess Gonchor |
| *Costume Design by* | Mary Zophres |

# Hail, Caesar!

*Fade in sound: distant voices.*

*Male voices. A Gregorian chant.*

*We fade in on a crucifix in the apse of a church: a suffering Christ.*

*We cut to a close shot of a small silver cross on a rosary. The rosary is held in a man's lap next to a mouse-grey fedora. The light is dim. As we hear a panel sliding, more light wipes onto the rosary beads.*

*Wider on the man waiting in the confessional: middle-aged, tired.*

> VOICE

Son, it is so late.

> MAN

Yeah, Father, work has just been . . .

> VOICE

You work too hard.

> MAN

Nah, I'm just . . . keepin' the place goin'. Anyhow, bless me, Father, for I have sinned. It's been uh, twenty-four hours since my last confession. I, uh . . .

> VOICE

Yes, my son.

> MAN

I lied to Connie. Uh, to my wife.

> VOICE

This is very serious.

> MAN

I know! I promised her I'd quit smoking. She thinks it's bad for me. And I'm trying, but . . . well, I snuck a couple of cigarettes. Maybe three.

VOICE
Yes.

MAN

It's hard.

VOICE

Yes, my son.

MAN

But I'm trying.

*A clap of thunder.*

HOUSE AT NIGHT

*We are looking – through the rain-pelted windshield of a parked car – at a small, Spanish-style bungalow. The rattle of driving rain does not quite cover the sound from inside the house of drunken female laughter. There are occasional flashes of lightning outside, and occasional flashes of strobe light in the windows of the house.*

*Inside our surveilling car a wrist rolls over to show a watch face, streaked with the shadows of dripping rain: five o'clock.*

*A voice-over begins, authoritatively omniscient – or maybe it only sounds so because it is British-accented:*

VOICE-OVER

It is 5:00 a.m., still shank of night for some – but for Eddie Mannix, the beginning of a new work day.

*Our car's driver, Eddie Mannix – the man we saw confessing – looks from his watch to the house.*

VOICE-OVER

The movie studio for which he works manufactures stories – each its own daylit drama, or moonlit dream.

*Flash of lightning, crash of thunder, another bout of laughter from the house.*

*Eddie Mannix reaches for his door.*

4

OUTSIDE

*Eddie Mannix emerges from his car – a Packard marking the period as circa 1950. Eddie pulls down his hat brim, turns up his collar, and digs hands into coat pockets as he strides through the rain.*

*The strobe light flashes inside the house. The laughter grows louder as we approach.*

*Eddie Mannix hesitates only momentarily at the front door. He tests the knob: unlocked; turns it, enters.*

> VOICE-OVER
> But the work of Eddie Mannix cares not for day or night . . . and cares little for his rest.


INSIDE THE HOUSE

*On Eddie Mannix at the open door, rain dripping from his fedora, thunder crashing behind him. His eyes narrow in distaste.*

*In the living room a giggling blonde in a milkmaid's dirndl with overloaded bodice bends over a butter-churn.*

*A man with his back to us is peering through a box camera.*

> MAN
> That's right, darlin', a little lower. . .

*The giggling girl sees Eddie Mannix and stops churning.*

> GLORIA
> Oh, fer – ecce homo! You, *here*?!

*The photographer turns to face Eddie: a tall weedy-looking man with a thin mustache. A sheen of sweat shines on his brow and upper lip.*

> EDDIE
> The studio has a right to Gloria's likeness, Falco. Gimme the negatives and things'll go easier.

> FALCO
> You got it all wrong, Eddie! This is f'private use!

*Eddie Mannix strides to the camera, pops its back and pulls out a length of film.*

FALCO

Hey!

*We hear approaching sirens. Falco reacts, bolting for the back door.*

GLORIA

Can't a girl take a few pitchas, have a few laughs? Cheez, Eddie, what a old stick-in-the-mud!

*She giggles.*

*Whap! He slaps her.*

*She looks at him, stunned, then starts weeping.*

*He slaps her again.*

*Outside the sirens wind down and we hear car doors open.*

EDDIE

Now you listen to me. You were at a party, you had too much to drink, somebody brought you here, you don't remember who. You're going home now and your name is Mary Jo Scheinbrotte.

*She blubbers:*

GLORIA

Okay, Eddie.

*The front door opens and two uniformed cops enter.*

COP ONE

Hello, Mannix, saw your heap outside.

COP TWO

Got a call. Loud, disorderly . . . (*Looks around, sniffs.*) Possible French postcard situation.

EDDIE

Someone was pulling your leg. Mary Jo here was just at a costume party. It's not really her dirndl.

*He fishes a wad from his pocket and peels off some bills.*

. . . She wants to contribute something to your pension fund. Sorry to drag you out in the rain, boys.

> COP ONE

Well, say, no trouble at all.

*Cop Two is looking hard at the girl.*

> COP TWO

Aren't you Gloria DeLamour?

> GLORIA

No no, I'm Mary Jo . . . somethin'.

> EDDIE

Scheinbrotte. Look, Brian . . .

*He hesitates, looking at one of the cops who is smoking. We hear, distantly but growing louder, a deep thumping sound.*

Can I, uh . . . bum a cigarette?

*The thumping sound has grown closer: the tramp of many marching feet. A fanfare on ancient horns as we cut to:*


THE OLD APPIAN WAY

*Down the road a Roman legion marches in brilliant Technicolor, the sound of its stamping feet bridging the cut. Cypress trees, regularly planted, stretch along either side of the road to the horizon. The title of the movie fades into superimposition:*

HAIL, CAESAR!
A Tale of the Christ

*The same voice that started the movie now intones:*

> VOICE-OVER

Ancient Rome! Twelve years into the rule of Tiberius, Rome's legions are masters of the world, the stomp of its sandals heard from the Iberian peninsula in the west through the halls of the great library of Alexandria in the east! As oppressed people everywhere writhe under the Roman lash . . .

*The regularly formed legions in the van now give way to slaves being whipped along in the rear:*

> . . . master and slave, freeman and vassal, are united in one compulsory worship: the Emperor, Caesar, is Godhead – lord of every man's body and spirit! For those who will not submit, the galleys, the arenas, even crucifixion await! But there is a new wind, blowing from the east, from the dusty streets of Bethlehem, that will soon challenge the vast house of Caesar – that edifice wrought of brick and blood which now seems so secure!

*A chariot rolls into the foreground. Its driver is a muscular campaign-hardened man with Roman bangs. Beneath his copper breastplate he glistens with manly sweat. He wears a helmet topped by a bright red mohawk bristle, something like an upside-down floorwaxer. He is Autolochus Antoninus. He gazes off and smiles.*

*Another man gallops up on horseback and reins in next to him. This is Gracchus Gregorius, and he too wears the floorwaxing headwear of the Roman tribune.*

> AUTOLOCHUS
> There she is, Gracchus. And ah, what a beauty!

> GRACCHUS
> Aye, Autolochus! Rome! Suckled by a she-wolf and nurturing us her sons in turn.

> AUTOLOCHUS
> Tonight I bathe in Caracalla, and wash away the dust of three hundred miles of Frankish road! To Rome! To Rome!

*As he whips the chariot horses into motion we pan off to reveal the hilltop view of Rome before which the weary tribunes had halted.*

> VOICE-OVER
> Yes, to Rome! Glorious center of Caesar's rule!

PALESTINE – NIGHT

*A rutted rural road. A man in sandals and simple peasant garb and using a gnarled walking staff walks through rain, thunder and lightning.*

But far away, in Palestine. . .

*We are panning off the image to reveal that we have been looking at a screen in a small screening room.*

. . . another man is coming home. Saul, humble merchant of Tarsus, is about to be struck down by a vision.

*The continued pan brings us onto the screening room's one occupant, Eddie Mannix. After a quick furtive look around – meaningless since he is alone – he takes a cigarette from the ashtray next to him and sneaks a puff.*

SAUL
*(off, quavering)*
What thing is this?


CAPITOL BACKLOT

*Eddie Mannix strides across the great studio backlot where technicians mill and actors dressed in the wardrobe of different ages and genres lounge. His secretary Natalie follows at his elbow, struggling to keep up as she consults a notepad:*

NATALIE
– and Gloria DeLamour has been checked into Our Lady of Perpetual Rest to dry out. You have a 10:00 a.m. with Monsignor O'Reilly at the Wallace Beery Conference Room. He's bringing Lester Silkwood from the Legion of Catholic Decency and we've also invited Patriarch Vlassos for the Eastern view.

EDDIE
They've read the script?

NATALIE
Roger.

EDDIE
Let's also invite a rabbi, and a protestant padre of some sort so we can get everybody's two cents.

NATALIE
Check.

EDDIE

How's production on *Tucumcari!*?

NATALIE

Principal is on schedule but second unit has been idle in
Gallup, New Mexico, for four days. Heavy rain.

EDDIE

Forecast?

NATALIE

Not good.

EDDIE

Hnn. Send an insert truck and have 'em shoot driving
plates for *Came the Rain*.

NATALIE

Check.

EDDIE

*Jonah's Daughter* still behind?

NATALIE

Yes, director says the problem is DeeAnna and she's
getting worse.

EDDIE

I know what it is, I'll drop in on her after my ten o'clock.
(*Pulls back his sleeve to look at his watch.*) All right, let's call
New York.


EDDIE'S OFFICE

*Eddie is on the phone.*

VOICE

Nick Schenk's office.

EDDIE

Hi, Dorothy, Eddie Mannix. The old man in?

VOICE

Hi, Mr. Mannix, I'll check.

*Eddie raises his voice:*

EDDIE

Natalie, I want the box office on *The Debonaires* and on
*Blessed Event*. Can you also – (*Hastily into the phone,
responding to voice.*) Yes, good morning Mr. Schenk! . . .
Very well, thank you. Proceeding . . . Proceeding . . .
*Merrily We Dance* starts shooting today. Beardley Auberon
gave us a draft that's extremely classy. Joan Van Vechten is
playing Dierdre, but we need a male lead and we need
him now . . . No, Jack Hogarth is drying out at Cedars . . .
Metro won't lend us Gable unless we give them the
Comiskey Twins . . . Of course not, I agree . . . Swell idea
but he's waiting out a divorce in Reno . . . Whuh – Hobie
Doyle?! Do you really think so? After all he's – he's a dust
actor! The man barely knows how to . . . talk! . . . Yes, of
course, Mr. Schenk, I agree, but I don't know if Hobie
Doyle, if he has the uh the uh the uh poise in a dinner
jacket . . . Yes, we do need someone pronto . . . No, I don't,
that's very true. Let me talk to Laurence Laurentz, the
director. It could work. Hobie is a very promising idea.

A BOULDER

*It is a great big boulder.*

*A beard-stubbled cowboy rises from behind its cover to fire his six-
shooter. He himself is immediately shot: he grimaces and releases his
gun which swivels around his trigger-finger, and he staggers – and
drops.*

*He who just shot him: Hobie Doyle, in white Western wear. Eyes
narrowed, he gauges the effect of his shot, then reacts to the sound
of retreating hoofbeats.*

*Other bad men are racing off, firing wildly back in his direction.*

*Hobie adroitly twirls and holsters his gun.*

HOBIE

Whitey!

*A white horse placidly cropping the grass several yards away flicks
its ears and looks over. It nickers and shuffles to face away from
Hobie as he runs to it. Hobie vaults its rump and man and animal
are off.*

*Hobie riding. A mounted bad man falls in behind him – a bushwhack. This pursuer begins to fire.*

*Hobie rocks forward on Whitey, low to his neck. He reaches down to grab the saddle, one hand on either side. He pushes himself up into a handstand atop the racing horse.*

*An oncoming tree limb hooks his knees and he swings up and around as his horse races on unridered. When he loops back around the tree limb his six-shooter is at the ready and he fires on the swing at the oncoming horseman. The bad man clutches his chest and falls from his horse as Hobie swings up again.*

*Hobie uses his upward inertia to gracefully execute a trapeze-artist dismount from the branch. His drop toward the ground is neatly intercepted by the bad man's galloping horse, Hobie plopping into its saddle. He reins in the snorting beast and as it rears he fires his six-shooter into the air in an expression of pure brio. He then twirls and holsters his gun, calms the horse with a pat on the neck, and leaps aground. He claps dust from his yoked white shirt.*

MEGAPHONE VOICE

And cut.

*A man in sunglasses rises from a canvas chair next to a camera attended by men in creased hoist-up pants and white shirts and ties.*

DIRECTOR

Great, Hobie.

HOBIE

I kin do the handstand smoother if ya gimme another shot atter.

DIRECTOR

We've got four good ones, Hobie, and Whitey is tired.

*An assistant trots up to Hobie with a small tin. Hobie takes it and loads a chew into one cheek.*

HOBIE

Okay, you're the bossman. If that's lunch ammo grab me a plate a beans.

ASSISTANT

Hobie, the studio wants you to escort Carlotta Valdez to your premiere tonight.

HOBIE

But she warn't in the pitcher.

ASSISTANT

Well, that's what they want.

HOBIE

But she warn't in the pitcher.

ASSISTANT

Well, it's some publicity thing.

HOBIE

Ah don't git it.

SISTANT

Well, the studio says you're bringing Carlotta Valdez. You're her escort.

HOBIE

But she's Carlotta Valdez. Hit don't make sense. She warn't in the pitcher.

ASSISTANT.

Who was in the picture?

*Hobie thinks.*

HOBIE

Whitey.

ASSISTANT

Well, Eddie Mannix says you're escorting Carlotta Valdez. They're changing your image.


ROMANS

*They sit in the courtyard of a Roman villa – several togaed senators and their robed wives – on chairs carved of cedar and draped with fine silks.*

13

*Incongruous entrance: a man in sunglasses wearing a white open-necked shirt.*

*He looks here and there. He raises a megaphone.*

1ST A.D.

All right, kids, it's Rome, you're over at this guy's house for a revel, and here comes Antoninus. Llllots of energy!

VOICE

Roll 'em.

*A short, togaed extra holding a lyre lurks by a tabletop on which sit platters of succulent feastings, and one goblet. A furtive look around.*

A.C.VOICE

Camera speed.

BOOM VOICE

Sound speed.

*The extra produces a cellophane packet from the folds of his toga. After another quick glance around he opens the packet's flap and taps its powdery contents into the goblet. He hastily crumples the packet and exchanges a significant look with:*

*Another extra, holding a turkey leg nearby. This man is bald with fringe hair upcombed to make corner hair-vees.*

*The first extra is startled by:*

1ST A.D.

What're you doing at the table of viands?!

EXTRA

. . . Huh?

1ST A.D.

You're supposed to be reclining, with the lyre!

EXTRA

Yeah, sorry, I uh –

1ST A.D.

Recline with the lyre!

EXTRA

Yes, sir.

VOICE

We set there? Background set?

1ST A.D.

Don't sit on the pediment! Recline! Relaxed, festive!

EXTRA

Yes, sir.

1ST A.D.
(*projecting*)

Set!

*Narrows his eyes and points at the extra now reclining, hissing as he leaves:*

I got my eye on you.

VOICE

Fountain!

*Water starts to gurgle as the courtyard fountain comes to life.*

VOICE

Background!

*The extras talk among themselves in pantomime, displaying Roman gaiety and deep involvement in their silent conversations. Some sip at goblets, some nibble at rich comestibles. Occasionally, a guest tips back his head for a peal of silent laughter.*

*Our extra strums his lyre not in pantomime but sounding it, the same arpeggio, over and over, separated by the same beat of silence.*

DIRECTOR

And action!

*Autolochus strides in. A senator rises to greet him.*

SENATOR

Autolochus! I had heard rumors of your return to Rome!

*We are close on the reclining extra with the lyre. Autolochus, standing before him, is only a pair of foreground feet in sandals with leather lace-ups twining the calves. The leather creaks as he talks:*

AUTOLOCHUS

More than rumors, noble Sestimus!

*The reclining extra looks steeply up at Autolochus. His point-of-view shows Autolochus mostly backlit; we see off the set and up into the greens.*

*Autolochus, with great aplomb, swipes the goblet from the table.*

> AUTOLOCHUS
> I see that you are the same worshipper of Bacchus. What gaiety! There is still truth in the adage, 'What pleasures cannot be found in the villa of Sestimus Amydias, cannot be found in Rome!' (*Brings the goblet to his lips but stops with a thought.*) But seriously. There is talk that the Senate will send our legions out again – and this time not on a short march to Gaul. What truth to these mutterings, Sestimus?

*The reclining extra and the extra with the turkey leg exchange a worried look.*

> SESTIMUS
> The matter is to be taken up in the Senate. It seems that there is unrest in Palestine.

> AUTOLOCHUS
> Palestine! That backwater! They'll hardly be sending the Sixth Legion to that godforsaken patch of desert!

*Hearty male laughter. Autolochus ends his laugh and raises the goblet to his lips.*

*Just before drinking – he is taken by another gust of laughter.*

*The two extras exchange a look. The reclining extra hugs his lyre and worriedly arpeggiates.*

*When Autolochus's second access of laughter peters out he raises the goblet again – and now takes a long draught.*

> DIRECTOR
> Holding for a dissolve . . . still laughing . . . holding . . . and . . . cut.

*Autolochus lowers the goblet, panting, and wipes meadfoam from his mouth with an armful of sleeve.*

*The extras relax.*

*The director enters: Sam Stampfel, of manly middle age.*

STAMPFEL
Fine, boys, that was fine. We'll move on to the brasier scene.

AUTOLOCHUS
Yeah? Was I okay on 'What truth to these mutterings?' I felt a little –

STAMPFEL
Nah, fine, we move on. Brasier scene, twenty minutes.

AUTOLOCHUS
Popping over to my dressing room. (*To Script Supervisor.*) Got the pages for the brasier scene?

*The Script Supervisor points to a spot on the page as she hands it over.*

SCRIPT SUPERVISOR
They changed 'passion' to 'ardor.'

AUTOLOCHUS
What?! I *liked* passion. It's strong. '*Passion.*'

*The Script Supervisor shrugs a what-can-I-tell-you. Autolochus wanders off, muttering:*

AUTOLOCHUS
Not so, Ursulina . . . My ardor is yet as warm as the embers of this brasier . . .

*The extra with the lyre exchanges another look with the bald extra. He indicates with a jerk of the head that they should follow Autolochus who, as he examines his script, is crossing the long dark expanse of soundstage, toward a distant glowing exit sign.*


CAPITOL BACKLOT

*Outside now, the short extra cautiously leans and cranes to peek around a soundstage corner. The bald extra is next to him.*

*His point-of-view: huge stucco soundstages range into the distance. The only person about is a small receding Autolochus Antoninus, his*

*sandals scuffing the road and sword banging his thigh as he walks.*
*He still looks at the script; we hear his distant muttering:*

> AUTOLOCHUS
> Such is my greeting after three months' sojourn in
> Gaul? . . . Not so, Ursulina . . . My ardor is yet as warm –

*He stops momentarily, swaying. He extends a hand to steady himself*
*against the exterior wall of a soundstage. After a moment, he moves*
*on, somewhat uncertainly.*

A STAR ON A DRESSING ROOM DOOR

*A slow pull back reveals the name above the star:* BAIRD
WHITLOCK.

*Muffled, from within, we hear Autolochus/Baird Whitlock:*

> BAIRD
> Not so, Ursulina. My ardor is yet as warm as the embers
> of this brasier . . . The embers of thish brasier . . .
> Goddamn, that's tough. Yet as warm as the embersh of
> this brasier . . . Not so, Urshulina. . .

*The continuing pull back reveals the two extras standing either side*
*of the door. The bald one nods at the short one.*

*At the nod, the short extra knocks.*

> SHORT EXTRA
> They're ready for you, Mr. Whitlock.

*The two men stand tensed.*

*After a short beat of clomping inside, the door swings slowly open.*
*Baird stands, swaying, giving the two men a glassy stare.*

> BAIRD
> (*slurred*)
> Not so, Ursulina –

*He pitches forward into the ready arms of the togaed men.*

CAPITOL CONFERENCE ROOM

*Eddie Mannix strolls and speaks. His audience is a four-person convocation of clergy sporting different hats, caps, robes, beards.*

> EDDIE
>
> Gentlemen, thank you all for coming. I know you have parishes, flocks and temples making enormous demands on your time. But I'm sure you appreciate also that great masses of humanity look to pictures for information and uplift and, yes, entertainment. Now here at Capitol Pictures, as you know, an army of technicians and actors and top-notch artistic people are working hard to bring to the screen the story of the Christ. It's a swell story – a story told before, yes, but we like to flatter ourselves that it's never been told with this kind of distinction and panache.

> EASTERN ORTHODOX PATRIARCH
>
> Perhaps, sir, you forget its telling in the Holy Bible.

*A wry smile from Eddie Mannix.*

> EDDIE
>
> Quite right, Padre. The Bible of course is terrific. But for millions of people, pictures will be their reference point for the story – the story's embodiment . . . (*groping*) the story's . . .

> MINISTER
>
> Realization.

*Eddie points an aiming finger at the Minister, saluting his choice of word.*

> EDDIE
>
> Realization.

> RABBI
>
> You 'realize,' of course, that for we Jews, any visual depiction of the Godhead is most strictly prohibited.

> EDDIE
> (*dismayed*)
>
> Oh.

RABBI

But of course, for us, the man Jesus Nazarene is not God.

EDDIE
(*brightening*)

Ah-ha.

MINISTER

Who plays Christ?

EDDIE

A kid we're all very excited about, Todd Hocheiser, wonderful young actor we found in Akron, Ohio, in a nationwide talent hunt. But Hocheiser is seen only fleetingly, and with extreme taste; our story is told through the eyes of a Roman tribune, Autolochus Antoninus, an ordinary man skeptical at first but who comes to a grudging respect for this swell figure from the East. And Autolochus is played by . . .

*He permits himself a satisfied smile.*

. . . Baird Whitlock.

*Murmurs of appreciation from the assembled and one low 'that's something' whistle.*

RABBI

Well, he is certainly a great talent.

EDDIE

Now *Hail, Caesar!* is a prestige picture, our biggest release of the year, and we are devoting huge resources to its production in order to make it first class in every respect. Gentlemen, given its enormous expense we don't want to send it to market except in the certainty that it will not offend any reasonable American, regardless of faith or creed. Now that's where you come in. You've read the script; I wanna know if the theological elements of the story are up to snuff.

PATRIARCH

I thought the chariot scene was fakey. How is he going to jump from one chariot to the other, going full speed?

*A frozen beat as Eddie frames an answer.*

Uh-huh, well, we can look at that. But as for the, uh,
religious aspect – does the depiction of Christ Jesus cut
the mustard?

PRIEST

The nature of the Christ is not quite as simple as your
photoplay would have it.

EDDIE

How so, Father?

FATHER

Well, it is not the case simply that Christ is God, or God
Christ.

RABBI

You can say that again! The Nazarene was not God!

PATRIARCH

He was not not-God.

RABBI

He was a man!

MINISTER

Part God.

RABBI

Nossir!

EDDIE

But Rabbi, we all have a little bit of God in us, don't we?

RABBI

Well . . .

PRIEST

It is the foundation of our belief that God is tripartite.

EDDIE

Father, Son, Holy Ghost.

PRIEST

And Christ is most properly referred to as the Son of
God. It is the son of God who takes the sins of the world

upon himself so that the rest of God's children, we imperfect beings, through faith, may enter the kingdom of heaven.

                        EDDIE
So God is . . . split?

                        PRIEST
Yes.

*Eddie nods.*

. . . And no!

*Eddie frowns.*

                        PATRIARCH
There is unity in division.

                        MINISTER
And division in unity.

                        EDDIE
Not sure I follow, Padre.

                        RABBI
Young man, you don't follow for a very simple reason: these men are screwballs. (*To the others.*) God has children? What, and a dog? A collie maybe? God doesn't have children. He's a bachelor. And very angry.

                        PRIEST
He *used* to be angry!

                        RABBI
What, he got over it?

                        MINISTER
You worship the god of another age!

                        PRIEST
Who has no love!

                        RABBI
Not true! He likes Jews.

MINISTER

God loves everyone!

PRIEST

God *is* love.

PATRIARCH

God is who is.

RABBI

This is special? Who isn't who is?

PRIEST

But how should God be rendered in a motion picture?

RABBI

God is not in the motion picture!

MINISTER

Then who's Todd Hocheiser?

EDDIE

Gentlemen, maybe we're biting off more than we can
chew. We don't need to agree on the nature of the deity:
if we can focus on the Christ, whatever his, uh, parentage.
My question is: is our depiction fair?

PATRIARCH

I've seen worse.

EDDIE

So I can put you in the plus column, Patriarch?

*The Patriarch gives a musing nod. Eddie turns to the Minister.*

. . . Reverend?

MINISTER

There is nothing to offend a reasonable man.

EDDIE

Father?

PRIEST

The motion picture teleplay was respectful and exhibited
tastefulness and class.

> RABBI

Who made you an expert all of a sudden?!

*Eddie turns wearily to the Jew.*

> EDDIE

. . . And what do you think, Rabbi?

*The Rabbi shrugs and affects mildness.*

> RABBI

Eh. I haven't an opinion.

CONFERENCE ROOM DOOR

*Eddie Mannix emerges, dabbing at sweat.*

> NATALIE

How'd we do?

> EDDIE

Mm. What's up?

> NATALIE

Can't find Baird Whitlock. He left the set over an hour ago, said he was going to his dressing room but he isn't there.

> EDDIE

Out on a bender? Am I crazy, middle of the day?

> NATALIE

You're not crazy, but no. I checked the Til Two, Dan Tana's, Rusty Scupper. No soap.

> EDDIE

Home, maybe? Called his wife?

> NATALIE

Yep.

> EDDIE

What'd Laura say?

> NATALIE

He's not home, he's never home, he's a louse, try one of his chippies.

EDDIE

Called that script girl, what's her name – Francie?

NATALIE

Check.

EDDIE

Any of the gals missing from the set?

NATALIE

Nope.

EDDIE

Well . . . (*Looks at his watch.*) Gone an hour? We won't worry yet.


TRUCK INTERIOR

*Baird Whitlock's head lolls in the foreground, waggling with the motion of the vehicle. His body – he is still in wardrobe, leather skirt and a breastplate over his white tunic – stretches away into the background: he is laid out, unconscious, on a paddywagon-style bench. At the end of the bench in the background we see, cropped and soft, a goon in a double-breasted suit, his forearms on his knees, smoking.*


THE STREET

*Hollywood Boulevard. The truck roars by. Its paneled side says 'Al's Linens.'*


STUDIO GATE

*Hobie Doyle is pulling up in a chauffeured car. The guard looks in the back window and is surprised to see the Western star.*

GUARD

How ya doing, Hobie.

HOBIE

Lo there, Scotty.

GUARD

They got you shooting on the lot?

Wul, Mr. Mannix pulled me off the Western, says I'm
doin' a movie on a soundstage. They built a drawing room.

GUARD

Ya don't say.


UNDER WATER

*A bathing beauty in a sequined mermaid suit swims free-armed
but wriggle-tailed, constrained by her fake nether-parts. From our
underwater perspective we hear burbling music.*

*After a beat of her swimming solo many bodies shoot down into the
water to join the Mermaid, entering foreground and background in
head-first dives that leave bubble trails. The beauties swim loops and
then wave themselves back up toward the surface, smiling.*

*But the Mermaid remains. She approaches a foreground sunken
treasure chest. Atop its gold coins sits a silver crown which the
mermaid seems to recognize as her own. She reaches for it, smiling –
but as she does so a shadow travels over her, near-to-deep. And then
great jaws hinge closed behind her, capturing her – and the lens – in
the black belly of a whale.*

*We linger in black. Water surface slowly emerges from the black: we
are high above the water now, looking straight down. With our
change in perspective the music now blares undistorted.*

*In the tank below us the bathing beauties spin in a formation that
goes through constant kaleidoscopic change. In the center of the
circle formed by the beauties a dark shape begins to resolve itself:
something is surfacing amid the girls.*

*It is the whale. As it breaches amid the swimmers its blowhole,
directly beneath the lens, spouts. Jetting water rises toward us.*

*Something else is rising, borne up by the jetting water: a sundae-cup
coach of sorts. In it rides the Mermaid, triumphantly ascending.*

*Her ascent ends high, high, high above the tank. The spouting water
recedes but her sundae cup remains magically suspended in air.*

*She opens the cup's gate-door and looks down at the water, far, far
below. As a drum roll builds she prepares to dive.*

26

*And does dive.*

*She splashes into the water and is lost from view. A suspenseful hold, on nothing.*

*And now she emerges from the water, rising again, now on a pedestal and now wearing her silver crown, recovered in what offscreen Neptunian rite who can say.*

*The Mermaid is proud of herself, proud of her crown, proud of her bathing-beauty minions – but then pride evaporates. Some internal struggle. She seems to be getting angry.*

*She yanks off the crown and tosses it away, squalling:*

MERMAID

Wardrobe!

*The music slows to sludge and stops.*

*The Mermaid flops into the water and splashes awkwardly toward the side of the tank, her fluke spanking the surface as cowed bathing beauties make way and an off-mike voice yells 'Cut!'*


CLOSE ON MERMAID

*A minute later: she is leaning back on a canvas chair, her face set in a grimace, a gurgle of effort building in her throat. Two men behind hold her in place, each with an arm looped over her shoulder and under an armpit.*

*After a long straining moment:*

MERMAID

GAH!

*With her cry there is a rubbery thwop-sound of suction giving way, and we cut to the reverse:*

*A stagehand staggers back, holding the now freed bottom half of her scaly mermaid outfit. He tips it backfin-upward and a little water dribbles out.*

*The Mermaid is now wearing the scaly top-half of her outfit only. Coming from beneath it, below her waist, is a conventional Catalina swimsuit. She feels tenderly at her stomach as an assistant director enters.*

A.D.

Gas again, ma'am?

MERMAID

MA'AM? MISS! Am I married?

A.D.

No, miss.

MERMAID

No. Yeah, sure, gas again.

*Eddie approaches. She indicates him.*

Ask him, he knows. Okay, scram.

EDDIE

How are you, DeeAnna?

DEEANNA

How am I? Wet. And I don't think I'll fit in the fish-ass after this week.

EDDIE

Well, we should have the water ballet in the can after tomorrow; in the nightclub scene wardrobe'll have a gown for you that's more . . . forgiving. Any more thoughts about who you might marry?

DEEANNA

HAH! Ain't doin' that again! I had two marriages, and it just cost the studio a lotta money to bust 'em up.

EDDIE

Well, we had to have those anulled – one was to a minor mob figure and –

DEEANNA

Vince was not *minor*!

EDDIE

And Buddy Flynn was a bandleader with a long history of narcotic use.

DEEANNA

Yeah yeah, they were both louses, yes, and that's what I'm sayin'. A third louse ain't gonnna do me no good.

28

EDDIE

We've offered you some very suitable, clean young men.

DEEANNA

Pretty boys, saps, and swishes! You think if there was
some good steady reliable man I wouldna grabbed him?

EDDIE

Well, what about Ärne Seslum? He is the father, isn't he?

DEEANNA

Yeah yeah.

EDDIE

The marriage doesn't have to last forever. But DeeAnna,
having a child without a father would present a public
relations problem for the studio. The aquatic pictures do
very nicely for us, and –

DEEANNA

So *you* strap on the fish-ass and marry Ärne Seslum!

EDDIE

The pictures do well for all of us. And it's a tribute to
you: the public loves you because they know how
innocent you are. Let me see if Ärne is open to, um . . .
matrimony. You're sure he's the father?

DEEANNA

Yeah yeah. Absolutely. He's the father, yeah . . . Pretty
sure.

*Eddie has been nodding and making to withdraw. The last sentence
gives him pause but DeeAnna, ready to get back to work, projects:*

. . . Okay Maxie, bring me my ass back!


COAST HIGHWAY

*The 'Al's Linens' truck rattles by. We hear the crash of surf.*

*Up ahead, on the right side of the road is a weathered sign for
'Rudy's Fish Shack – 500 yards.' Just before the sign is a turn-off
to the left, onto an unpaved and rutted road. The truck makes the
left turn.*

DRAWING ROOM

*People in formal-wear lounge, chatting.*

*Hobie Doyle enters stiffly in a tuxedo. He tugs at his collar.*

*A distinguished-looking man, middle-aged, well dressed but not in wardrobe, hastens to greet Hobie. He is the director, Laurence Laurentz.*

LAURENCE LAURENTZ
My dear boy, you look wonderful, how do you feel?

HOBIE
Well, this here collar is a little tight.

LAURENCE LAURENTZ
No no, nicely fit, looks a marvel, just takes a little getting used to. Now you enter here, Hobie, having just seen Biff's valise in the foyer – in spite of Allegra's claim that he hasn't been to the house.

HOBIE
I'm sweet on Allegra.

LAURENCE LAURENTZ
Indeed you are.

HOBIE
But I seen Biff's grip.

LAURENCE LAURENTZ
Indeed you have. And so here we find you haunted by unspoken suspicions.

HOBIE
Haunted. By Biff's grip.

LAURENCE LAURENTZ
By his valise, yes, but then here is Dierdre . . .

*He indicates an actress on the couch who coldly examines Hobie – a veteran with no patience for rookies.*

. . . harboring deep feelings for you, and sensing opportunity.

HOBIE

Dierdre.

LAURENCE LAURENTZ

Dierdre, yes. So at her importuning, you join her on the couch, and conversation ensues.

HOBIE
(*troubled*)

So now she's gonna importune, Mr. Laurence?

LAURENCE LAURENTZ

Laurentz.

HOBIE

Oh, I'm sorry. She's gonna importune? Is that somethin' I should, uh, be concerned about –

LAURENCE LAURENTZ

She'll simply ask you to join her on the couch, is all I mean to say, and conversation ensues.

HOBIE

Okay, I gotcha.

LAURENCE LAURENTZ

Very good, very good, let's try one shall we?

HOBIE

Sure, I'll give her a go.

LAURENCE LAURENTZ

Wonderful, splendid. (*Turns away but turns back with a thought.*) The only thing I would suggest is, before your first line, you respond to her line with a mirthless chuckle.

HOBIE

A mirthless chuckle.

LAURENCE LAURENTZ

Yes, given your unspoken suspicions about Allegra, a mirthless chuckle.

HOBIE

Okay, Mr. Laurence, I'll give it a –

Laurentz.

                        HOBIE
Oh, gosh, I'm sorry, Mr. Laurentz. I'll give it a shot.


THROUGH FILM

*A clapper-boy ID's and whacks a slate on 'Merrily We Dance.'*

*Laurence Laurentz's voice calls 'Action!'*

*Those assembled in the parlor come to life in a pantomime of civilized conviviality, chatting and laughing.*

*Hobie enters, an uneasy backward glance referring perhaps to the unseen grip.*

                        DIERDRE
Oh, Monty! Come join me on the divan!

*Briefest who-me confusion from Hobie. With a quick recovery he manages a fairly casual saunter to the couch where he plants himself – not close to Dierdre. She slides over to close the gap between them, and is now all warmth and sympathy. Her voice is musical and upper-crust:*

                        DIERDRE
It seems Allegra's a no-show, which is simply a bore, but I can partner you in bridge. (*Reacting to him.*) Why the pout?

*Gazing at the floor, Hobie gives a short loud laugh that sounds like a Heimlich-expulsion. A flinch from the actress. Hobie's grin abruptly drops, and, still gazing at the floor:*

                        HOBIE
Would that it were sooooo . . . simple.

*A beat, the actress looking at him, Hobie looking at the floor.*

*The beat grows longer . . . longer . . .*

*Voice of Laurence Laurentz: 'Cut!'*

*We cut to Laurence Laurentz in his director's chair, mouth slightly open, staring without expression as he tries to frame his notes.*

*He abruptly rises and walks into the set to join Hobie.*

> LAURENCE LAURENTZ
>
> Very good – wonderful in fact. But let's try it a little
> differently this time –

> HOBIE
>
> Sure.

> LAURENCE LAURENTZ
>
> – let's try, well, let's see, first of all why don't we dispense
> with the mirthless chuckle.

> HOBIE
>
> *No* mirthless chuckle.

> LAURENCE LAURENTZ
>
> No, no need, really – it was a bad idea, bad directorial –
> my fault, overthinking the thing.

> HOBIE
>
> Well, if you say so, but I'm happy to do another – maybe
> try her one more time – I mean if you want that chuckle
> I sure wanna give her to ya –

> LAURENCE LAURENTZ
>
> No no no, completely unnecessary under the circum-
> stances, I think the audience can to that extent read your
> thoughts, and will assume your mirthlessness.

> HOBIE
>
> Okay, you're the bossman, Mr. Laurence.

> LAURENCE LAURENTZ
>
> Laurentz.

> HOBIE
>
> Oh, gosh, I'm sorry, Mr. Laurentz –

> LAURENCE LAURENTZ
>
> Also, let's try, this time, actually looking at Dierdre as we
> speak, looking into her eyes, and speaking our line with a
> certain . . . ruefulness.

*Hobie nods agreement.*

HOBIE

Ruefulness, okay.

LAURENCE LAURENTZ

Yes. Because it's not so simple. Not so simple as she suggests.

HOBIE

Okay.

LAURENCE LAURENTZ

Your feelings are not so simple.

HOBIE

Nawsir. Okay.

LAURENCE LAURENTZ

Splendid.


THROUGH FILM

*A clapper-boy ID's and whacks a slate on 'Merrily We Dance' identifying the scene number and Take 2.*

*Laurence Laurentz's voice calls 'Action!'*

*Those assembled in the parlor come to life in a pantomime of civilized conviviality, chatting and laughing.*

*Hobie enters.*

DIERDRE

Oh, Monty! Come join me on the divan!

*Smoothly this time, Hobie joins her on the sofa. When he sits he is still not close; she slides to him. The same music in her intonation:*

DIERDRE

It seems Allegra's a no-show, which is simply a bore, but I can partner you in bridge. (*Reacting to him.*) Why the pout?

*Hobie looks at her, somewhat shifty-eyed, not comfortable with the eye contact.*

(*rueful*)
Would that? (*Slight beat; sad head-shake.*) It were soooo . . .
simple.

*Voice of Laurence Laurentz: 'Cut!'*

*Hobie looks hopefully to the approaching Laurence Laurentz. The
director, feeling his look, puts on a smile.*

LAURENCE LAURENTZ
Good, very good. Wonderful, in fact. Let's try, this time. . .

*He balls a fist and brings it to his mouth and stares at the floor,
thinking.*

*Hobie waits, gazing up at him.*

*At length:*

All right, let's try this, your line, just say it as I say it, say
your line exactly as I'm about to. Just as I'm about to do.

HOBIE
Sure, okay.

*Beat to focus attention, and then:*

LAURENCE LAURENTZ
(*rueful, and British-accented*)
Would that it'were so simple.

HOBIE
Would that ih twuuuuuuh, so simple.

*Laurence Laurentz stares at him.*

LAURENCE LAURENTZ
My dear boy, why do you say that – why do you say,
'twuuuuuh'?

HOBIE
Well you said, say it like I say it.

LAURENCE LAURENTZ
Yes but –

HOBIE

Would that it twuuuuuuh, so simple.

LAURENCE LAURENTZ

Would that it'were so simple.

HOBIE

Would that ih twuuuuuh, so simple.

LAURENCE LAURENTZ

Would that it'were so simple.

HOBIE

Okay, I'm tryin' to do that, Mr. Laurentz –

LAURENCE LAURENTZ

Laurence.

HOBIE

I thought – um, a minute ago it was Laurentz –

LAURENCE LAURENTZ

We can use Christian names, my good dear boy. Laurence
is fine –

HOBIE

Okay.

LAURENCE LAURENTZ

– just as I call you Hobie. So, 'Would that it'were so
simple.' Trippingly.

HOBIE

Would that it twuuuuh –

LAURENCE LAURENTZ

You seem to be lingering, it's interminable –

HOBIE

Oh gosh.

LAURENCE LAURENTZ

– I'm wondering when it'll end, the 'were,' and we
shouldn't have to wonder, should we, we should be
marching right along to 'so simple'!

HOBIE

Would that ih . . . (*after hesitating, rushed*) twersa*simple.*
Twersa*simple.*

LAURENCE LAURENTZ

Would that it were so simple. Not '*simple!*' Just . . .
(*relaxed*) simmple.

HOBIE

Simmmple. Simmmple. Gosh, I can't seem to cinch
m'saddle up on this'n, Larry –

LAURENCE LAURENTZ

Larry! Good God, Christian names, yes, but not Larry!


FROM A HIGH BLUFF

*We are looking down into a hidden box cove of the Pacific Ocean,
rugged and secluded. Surf pounds into the teeth of jagged rocks
offshore. Nestled in the canyon just above the cove's tiny beach is a
modernist octahedral beach house.*

*The 'Al's Linens' truck is parked where the beach road ends just in
front of the house. The goon from inside the truck now has Baird
Whitlock in a fireman's carry, taking him to the house's front door.*

*We jump down close – the surf louder here – as the goon knocks. The
knock brings furious dog-yapping from inside.*

*We are close on Baird's head upside-down against the big man's
back. Just past the two men the door swings open, and as the big
man steps in he turns to negotiate Baird's body through the
doorway, Baird's sandaled legs sweeping past us.*

*There are two men waiting inside. The one at the door is middle-
aged, with sad eyes. He is John Howard Herman.*

*The man deeper in the room is heavy-set, in a cheap suit not freshly
pressed. Near him, a springer spaniel frantically spins in place
yapping, excited to have visitors.*

MAN

Quiet, Engels!

*When the goon has passed with his Roman cargo, the sad-eyed
John Howard Herman swings the door toward us, filling the lens.*

*On the other side of Eddie's desk is producer Walt Dubrow.*

> DUBROW

Stall?! For how long? What do I tell the director?

> EDDIE

That we're looking for him. But we don't want it in the gossip columns – Baird on a bender or in a love nest or wherever we end up finding him. As far as the set is concerned it's business as usual. Tell the A.D. Baird is out briefly with a high ankle sprain.

> DUBROW

Fine, but what do we shoot without him? We got the brasier scene up this afternoon.

> EDDIE

Could you get through it shooting around him? – Maybe use his stunt double, Chunk Mulligan.

> DUBROW

Chunk can't act.

> EDDIE

Get the writer to trim his speeches.

> DUBROW

Well, maybe, but then what? All we got left is the final scene – Autolochus's speech at the feet of the penitent thief.

*Eddie grimaces.*

> EDDIE

Uh-huh.

> DUBROW

It's the emotional climax of the entire picture! We have to see that Autolochus has absorbed the message of the Christ!

> EDDIE

Yeah, I can see that.

DUBROW

We need Baird's star power, his charisma!

*A wave of Eddie's hand communicates the ineffable:*

EDDIE

Sure, his emotional, uh –

DUBROW

This can't be faked! This is the heart and soul of the picture!

EDDIE

I understand –

DUBROW

End of the movie, we can't give that speech to some – some – some Roman schmoe!

EDDIE

Yeah, yeah, I got it. But his benders can last a day or two – what does it cost to shut down?

DUBROW

Plenty. You know how big the picture is, we're on Stages 5 and 14, if we're carrying everybody in the last scene who's up on crucifixes that's three-forty an hour hardship pay eight hour minimum –

EDDIE

Yeah yeah. (*His phone buzzes. He punches the button.*) Not now.

DUBROW

– not to mention we lose Todd Hocheiser to Fox at the end of the week.

EDDIE

Shoulda made him exclusive; who knew. (*Another buzz from the phone.*) Not now!

NATALIE'S VOICE

It's Mr. Laurentz, Mr. Mannix! I can't stop him!

*The door bursts open and Laurence Laurentz storms in. Natalie has trailed him to the door, where she hovers.*

EDDIE

It's all right, Natalie. Okay, Walt, lemme know –

LAURENCE LAURENTZ

Mannix, I won't have it! For two decades the words
'Laurence Laurentz Presents' have meant something to
the public!

EDDIE

What's on your mind, uh . . . Laurence?

LAURENCE LAURENTZ

Hobie Doyle cannot act!

EDDIE

Hobart Doyle is one of the biggest movie stars in the
world.

LAURENCE LAURENTZ

On horseback! But this is drama, Mannix – real drama,
an adaptation of a Broadway smash! It requires the skills
of a trained thespian, not a rodeo clown. I begged you
for Lunt!

*Natalie has been hesitant to butt in:*

NATALIE

Mr. Mannix, I'm sorry but – you wanted me to make sure
you didn't miss your lunch at the Imperial Gardens. You
never told me who with.

EDDIE

Right. (*Looks at watch, grimaces.*) Nuts. Look: no one
wants to see Lunt. We're not recasting; this came from
Mr. Schenk himself: it's Hobie Doyle. Is the boy game?

LAURENCE LAURENTZ

Oh, he's game. And gamey!

EDDIE

If he needs help it's your job to help him. I'll have a talk
with Hobie and take a look at what you've shot – but
right now, I've got a lunch.

BLACK

*The pounding of surf fades up, close but muffled by interior perspective.*

*We are fading up on Baird Whitlock, lying on his back, still unconscious. He lies on a patio chaise lounge made of thin plastic tubing stretched across an aluminum frame. We are in a storeroom, the chaise being the room's only piece of furniture.*

*A muffled ding-dong from the front of the house. We hear the springer spaniel, stirred by the bell to yapping.*

*With much plastic-squeaking Baird rolls onto his side and nestles his head into the chaise's tubing-upholstery. In his sleep he murmurs:*

BAIRD

What truth to these mutterings, Sestimus . . .

*He subsides to snoring.*

MAIN ROOM

*The sad-eyed man, John Howard Herman, is opening the front door to several visitors. The first enters: murmured greetings, solemn handshake. Another man, another sober handshake. Then an elderly man in tweeds clutching a pipe, the greeting for him especially deferential. Then a man with a briefcase; he sets it down so that he may greet by means of a hug. He picks up the briefcase, makes way for the next man.*

*A counter separates the entryway from a small kitchen. In it, the man we saw shushing the dog when Baird was brought in is carefully cutting the crusts off of finger sandwiches and stacking them on a platter.*

*As the dog yaps in a frenzy of delight at all the visitors, the man reacts without looking up:*

MAN

Quiet, Engels!

*A gong stings the cut to the interior of this Chinese restaurant.*

*Arthur Fung, a grave-looking man in a dark suit and conservative tie, greets Eddie Mannix.*

ARTHUR FUNG

How pleasant to see you, Mr. Mannix, your table is right over here.

EDDIE

Thank you, Arthur.

*They splash through a curtain of beads to approach a booth at which another man sits, a drink with an umbrella before him, an ashtray and an Imperial Gardens matchbook next to it, a cigarette in his hand. He rises to shake.*

MAN

How ya doing, Mannix.

EDDIE

Mr. Cuddahy.

CUDDAHY

Mix a hell of a mai-tai. I like this place.

*The men seat themselves facing each other.*

EDDIE

Sorry to keep you hanging – it's a tough decision.

CUDDAHY

Nothing to apologize for – we said the offer was on the table for a week.

*Cuddahy has noted Eddie eyeing his cigarettes. He picks up the pack and offers with a hitch of the wrist that sends four cigarettes nosing out of the foil.*

CUDDAHY

Go ahead.

EDDIE

Nah, I'm . . . I've been trying to . . .

CUDDAHY

The deadline was tomorrow, but, frankly, we were
surprised not to get a quick yes. I just wanted to see if
there was some impediment we could help with, or if
something in the offer isn't clear?

EDDIE

The offer's very clear. And very generous.

CUDDAHY

We want to make it easy for you to say yes. Look, Mannix,
we need a guy with your talents in management, problem-
solving. And you need to think about the future. Lockheed
is booming – it's reflected in the offer we made you.
Everyone is riding in airplanes, and we're moving into jet
airplanes. It's a new age, Mannix, and we're part of it; the
industry you're in – what's the future there? What happens
when everybody owns a television set? Will they still be
going to pictures every week?

EDDIE

Well, we –

CUDDAHY

I don't mean to denigrate; I'm sure the picture business
is pretty damned interesting. But it's also pretty frivolous,
isn't it? Aviation is serious; serious business, serious
people. You won't be babysitting a bunch of oddballs and
misfits, shouldering a lot of crackpot problems from
people who –

EDDIE

Look, we have some kooks, sure –

CUDDAHY

Course they're kooks, it's all make-believe! (*Quick grimace
and smile. He leans back.*) I told myself I wasn't gonna
badmouth the competition, and looka me. Sorry, Mannix,
I'll stick to what we're about. Lemme show you something.
(*Digs in a pocket.*) Ever heard of the Bikini Atoll?

EDDIE

What?

CUDDAHY

It was a test site, couple of rocks in the South Pacific – till a few weeks ago. Then we blew the Aitch-erino. Not supposed to be telling you this. (*Hands Eddie a picture.*) The real world. Hydrogen bomb. Fusion device.

EDDIE

Armageddon.

CUDDAHY

And Lockheed was there. We had a –

*He cuts himself off. A splash of the bead curtain.*

WAITRESS

Call for you, Mr. Mannix.

*The waitress, in a red embroidered sheath dress, is entering with a telephone. She plugs it in. As she leans to set it on the table Cuddahy swipes the picture from Eddie's hand where it was exposed to view.*

EDDIE

Thank you . . . Hello? . . . And he has it now? . . . No, have him stay on set, I'll go to him. (*Slams down the phone and rises.*) Sorry, Cuddahy, work emergency. Still do work there, for the day anyway. (*Grabs his hat, calls back over his shoulder.*) You make a good case. I'll let you know.


MALIBU HOUSE

*There is a dull clunk and we are close on Baird Whitlock, who opens his eyes.*

*Wider: Baird in his centurion's wardrobe reclining on the beach chaise. The sound of the ocean outside.*

*The clunk has punctuated an ongoing machine hum which continues, cycling louder and softer, its loudest approach always punctuated by a clunk.*

*The lawn chair makes tacky noises as Baird disengages from it. He stiffly sits up. He gazes stupidly about, looking into the depth of the room: where am I?*

*He twists to look behind himself, lawn chair crackling, and does a modest take: out the window is the Pacific Ocean.*

*Another clunk and receding machine hum. Baird registers the noise, gets to his feet and walks to the door. It is closed. He reaches for the knob. He tries the knob. It turns. He goes through the door.*

LIVING ROOM

*The main room, in which we saw Baird being brought in and the mysterious visitors entering. It is now empty except for a middle-aged woman with a bandana tied Aunt Jemima-style on her head. She vacuums. Each forward pass of the machine ends with its clunk against the wall.*

*The woman looks up, but shows no particular interest in Baird despite his breastplate and leather skirt. She turns off the vacuum.*

> WOMAN
> You one of the Hollywood people?

*Baird stares at her, considering all the possible answers. Finally:*

> BAIRD
> . . . Maybe.

> WOMAN
> They're in there.

*A jerk of her head indicates a hallway. She fires up the machine again.*

*Baird looks down the hallway. From one of its rooms, muffled male laughter.*

*He goes cautiously down the hall, the vacuum sound fading away, male voices fading up. One door is ajar. Baird cautiously bumps it open further.*

*Another round of laughter is interrupted as all turn to look at the Roman-attired man in the doorway. Most of the interrupted party is seated; there are a couple of overflow standees; several men smoke cigarettes, one smokes a cigar; the tweedy elderly man is sunk back in an easy chair smoking his pipe.*

45

*The springer spaniel leaps and twists and yaps, excited by the new arrival.*

DOG SHUSHER

Quiet, Engels!

*Again, this does nothing to quiet the dog. Baird looks from man to man. John Howard Herman, the man who greeted the other arrivals at the door, the apparent host, waves Baird in.*

HERMAN

Please! Enter! All are welcome!

*Baird cautiously enters. One man vacates a seat for him.*

*Baird cautiously sits. His scabbard catches on the chair arm, prompting chuckles from some of the men.*

HERMAN

Those things are a nuisance!

*A nearby man leans over to help him adjust it. Baird sits back.*

BAIRD

Thank you. Uh . . .

*The men look to him, waiting for him to bring out his thought. Herman helps:*

HERMAN

Wondering where you are?

BAIRD

Yeah.

*The dog has subsided and comes over to sniff at Baird's sword.*

HERMAN

Malibu. We'll have sandwiches in a minute. Tea?

BAIRD

. . . Tea. Well. Okay. Okay. And . . . and –

HERMAN

And what's going on?

BAIRD

Yeah.

46

SECOND MAN

Well, we've just read the minutes and Allen was about to bring up new business.

BAIRD

So . . . I missed the minutes.

HERMAN

I wouldn't worry about it.

THIRD MAN

They're usually pretty boring.

BAIRD

Uh-huh. And – what kind of meeting – exactly –

HERMAN

Well it's not a 'meeting,' so much as a, a – what should we say?

BENEDICT

It's a – more of a, a study group.

BAIRD

And you're studying . . .?

HERMAN

Oh, all sorts of jolly stuff.

THIRD MAN

History.

DUTCH

Economics.

THIRD MAN

Same thing, isn't it – history, economics?

HERMAN

Don't you agree?

*All are looking at Baird.*

BAIRD

Well . . . I'm . . . I'm not really a student of history.

*Someone reaches in to take a sandwich off the offered platter.*

*Wider: Baird sits back with the finger sandwich. It is minutes later and the respectful quiet has now given way to the relaxed clatter of people eating, laughing, having side-conversations.*

> BAIRD

Thank you. So man is . . . split?

> HERMAN

Well, man's functions are split. There's the little guy, the regular Joe, who works for a living. He's the body, uh, body politic. Then there's the brain – the boss, the owner –

> SECOND MAN

The boss is not the brain!

> ANGRY MAN

No no! The boss is parasite!

> HERMAN

Well, it's true that the boss doesn't work, but he has a function in the system –

*Baird looks from man to man, as at a tennis match.*

He controls the means of –

> SECOND MAN

– production, sure, but that's not a function, that's, that's –

> ANGRY MAN

Parasitism! On the body! On the body politic! Of the regular Joe! It's –

*A throat-clearing.*

*Everyone instantly quiets. All look to the old man in tweeds who is just lowering his pipe. Having claimed the floor, he now speaks with non-argumentative authority.*

> MARCUSE

Man is unitary – a simple economic agent. Man's institutions are split, expressing contradictions that must be worked through. And they are worked through in a causative, predictable way: history is science. This is the essence of the dialectic.

*Click! A sallow, thin young man with heavy beard shadow has just snapped a picture of Baird. A sickly smile at Baird and then he turns to face someone else in the room and – click! – take another picture.*

HERMAN

See, if you understand economics, you can actually write down what will happen in the future, with as much confidence as you write down the history of the past. Because it's science. It's not make-believe. Like Professor Marcuse says. There's no mystery.

THIRD MAN

We don't believe in Santa Claus!

*Hearty guffaws.*

*Click! The photographer is edging around the group, continuing his picture-taking.*

HERMAN

Another finger sandwich? More tea?

BAIRD

But if I – sure, thank you – if I follow this, correctly, you – (*Eye caught by man with camera.*) Who's he?

SECOND MAN

Mr. Smitrovich takes pictures for our newsletter.

*The sallow picture-snapper smiles again at Baird.*

MARCUSE

Our understanding of the true workings of history gives us access to the levers of power. Your studio, for instance, is a pure instrument of capitalism. As such it expresses the contradictions of capitalism, and can be enlisted to finance its own destruction.

HERMAN

Which is exciting! It can be made to help the little guy, the regular Joe –

ANGRY MAN

The body politic!

HERMAN

Shut up! – help the little guy, even though its purpose is
to exploit the little guy.

BAIRD

Okay, so you guys are for the little guy.

HERMAN

Well – for the little guy, against – it doesn't matter,
history will be what it will be and we already know what
it will be, but – yes, we're for the little guy, aren't you?

BAIRD

Are you joking? Me, for the little guy? Of course I'm for
the little guy! Is this guy a comedian?

FOURTH MAN

And you would act. To help the little guy.

BAIRD

Act?

FOURTH MAN

Praxis.

BAIRD

What?

FOURTH MAN

Act.

BAIRD

Yeah yeah, act yeah, but – sorry fellas, this is good stuff,
but – I oughta get back to work, they must be goin' nuts.
Can we cut it off and pick it up right here at the next
study session?

*The clatter subsides to quiet. Cautious looks are exchanged among
the men.*

*Herman, gazing at Baird and nodding, thinking, finally formulates
his opening:*

HERMAN
Okay, well, see: I'm afraid it's not that simple.

*As we cut wide on the room, the same voice that narrated the sandal epic* Hail, Caesar! *at the beginning of our movie returns, distinguished, British-accented, authoritative yet plummily comforting:*

VOICE-OVER
And so Baird Whitlock found himself in the hands of Communists. . .

*Herman starts to silently explain things to Baird. The scene of cozy bonhomie is framed by the elemental vastness of the ocean outside.*

Meanwhile, far from the crashing surf of Malibu, Eddie Mannix, torn from his lunch with the Lockheed man . . .

CAPITOL LOT

*A montage of Eddie, a tiny, solitary figure, striding through the canyons between enormous sand-colored soundstages.*

. . . hurries back to the vastness of Capitol Pictures, whose tireless machinery clanks on, producing this week's ration of dreams for all the weary peoples of the world.

*Closer on Eddie as he enters the small door of a soundstage. The light above the door is flashing red.*

INSIDE

*High-ceilinged darkness and quiet. A man posted at the door hisses at Eddie, entering:*

MAN
Hey, numbskull, didn't you see the 'rolling' li— Oh, I'm sorry Mr. Mannix. Can I help you find someone?

*We have been hearing the distant, echoing voices of two actors, a hoarse-voiced man and a silken-voiced woman.*

*Their voices bump up full as we cut to the periphery of the scene being shot around a great flickering brasier. An actor in centurion's wardrobe identical to Baird's has one hand half-covering his face as the other arm stretches out as if to repel the gaze of a revealingly clad slavegirl.*

URSULINA

Autolochus! Why do you present yourself in my chambers in such humble fashion?

CHUNK MULLIGAN

Do not look upon me, Ursulina. The fires of the brasier of Sestimus latterly burned my face, though the unguents of Arkimideus promise shortly to undo the damage.

*In the foreground Eddie leans in to Walt Dubrow, watching the scene, and whispers:*

EDDIE

Walt.

DUBROW

Eddie!

*He fishes a twice-folded paper from his pocket.*

*Eddie holds it up so that he may read by the flickering gag-light that simulates brasier flames. Typewritten:*

> *We have your movie star.*
> *Gather $100,000 and await instructions.*
> *Who are We?*
> *The Future.*

URSULINA

You know that my love is for you not for your station, and neither does it care for the transitory blemishes that now mark your visage.

*Eddie gives a low whistle at the contents of the note.*

CHUNK MULLIGAN

And my ardor for you is yet as warm as the embersh of thish bra – goddamnit – this brazher. I'm sorry, goddamnit.

VOICE

Cut!

OUTSIDE

*Eddie and Walt emerge from the soundstage onto an exterior set with thick temple columns.*

> DUBROW
>
> Somebody slipped it under my door some time after we broke this morning.

> EDDIE
>
> Mention it to anyone?

> DUBROW
>
> Nope.

*Eddie gazes, unseeing, down the row of columns as two workmen tip the farthest one, striking it.*

> EDDIE
>
> Okay, let's keep it that way. (*Realizes where he is.*) We shot this out?

> DUBROW
>
> Chasing the money-lenders from the temple? Yeah, last Friday.

*Eddie nods, thinking.*

> EDDIE
>
> What do you think they mean, 'The Future'?

*Walt answers with a beats-me shrug and headshake. Eddie gazes back down at the note and moseys off – but turns back with a bright finger-cock at Walt:*

> . . . Chunk sounded good in there!


EDDIE'S OUTER OFFICE

*Eddie bangs through a door that says:*

> EDWARD MANNIX
> HEAD OF PHYSICAL PRODUCTION

> EDDIE
>
> Natalie, could you please get me Stu Schwartz, Accounting?

*Eddie strides in as the phone on his desk buzzes:*

NATALIE'S VOICE
Stu Schwartz on two.

EDDIE
Stu, how are you. I need some petty cash . . . Hundred
thousand. I'm sorry, did I say 'petty'? . . .

*With the handset shoulder-clamped to his ear he stoops and pulls an
attaché case from the legwell of his desk and places it on the desktop
and pops the clasps and starts emptying it.*

. . . Yeah, well it's a long story and I'll tell it to ya sometime.
You have that much in the office? . . . How much space'll
that take up? . . . Okay, this might do it. I'll be over in a
minute.

*As soon as he disconnects, Natalie edges into the office.*

NATALIE
Thora Thacker just came in, wonders if you have a
moment.

*Eddie winces.*

EDDIE
Thora Thacker. Tell her I'm stuck on a call. I'll leave
through the patio.


CAPITOL LOT

*As Eddie marches past the executive offices with his emptied attaché
case, a tall red-haired woman arcs in to march alongside him. He
winces.*

WOMAN
Call didn't take so long, then.

EDDIE
Yes – no – fast talker. What can I do for you, Thora?

THORA THACKER
Well, I'll be fast too. I only wanted to notify you as a
courtesy that I'm running my story on Baird Whitlock.

                              EDDIE
Yeah? What story?

                         THORA THACKER
*The* story. I have a credible source and I'm going to run it,
and I think you know what story I mean.

                              EDDIE
I have no idea – there's nothing going on with Baird. I
would know, wouldn't I?

                         THORA THACKER
Don't play dumb, Eddie, I'm talking about . . . (*dramatic
pause, dramatic delivery*) On Wings as Eagles.

*This stops Eddie in his tracks. He stares at Thora, wide-eyed and
shaken.*

*Finally:*

                              EDDIE
What?!

*She gives him a knowing look and a confirming nod.*

                         THORA THACKER
Running it tomorrow.

                              EDDIE
First of all – first of all – first of all – there's nothing to
that story. I've heard it, it's been around forever, and it's
never been confirmed. And secondly – you can't print
that! Even if you *could* print it you couldn't print it. And
you wouldn't want to, Thora, it's beneath you.

                         THORA THACKER
The facts are never beneath me.

                              EDDIE
People don't want the facts, they want to believe. That's
our great industry – mine, and yours too. They want to
believe that Baird Whitlock is a great star – and a good
man.

                         THORA THACKER
You're admitting he isn't.

EDDIE

No, I'm saying he is, though it's beside the point. There's nothing to it, nothing to the gossip.

THORA THACKER

I AM NOT A GOSSIP COLUMNIST!

EDDIE

No no, of course not –

THORA THACKER

Don't confuse me with my sister!

EDDIE

Hardly. But look – do you have to run it tomorrow?

THORA THACKER

It's my entire column. I'm happy to talk to Baird for comment, but it'll have to be this afternoon.

EDDIE

Baird is unavailable right now. Wait one day.

*A chirping hoot from Thora.*

*Eddie grimaces and lowers his voice confidentially:*

EDDIE

Thora, wait one day and I'll give you a true story for tomorrow's column. A little something – about Hobie Doyle.

THORA THACKER

My readers don't care about Hobie Doyle. He wears chaps.

EDDIE

Do they care about Carlotta Valdez? They're sweet on each other. You should see the two of 'em together, peas in a pod.

THORA THACKER

Trade the story of my career for a puff piece on Hobie Doyle? I don't think so.

EDDIE

You're not trading anything, you're waiting one day on a story that's years old. Give me a day, I can let you talk to Baird and show you your story's the bunk. And if I'm wrong, no skin off your nose, you run the column. In the meantime you have an exclusive – no one else knows about Hobie and Carlotta.

*Thora eyes him suspiciously.*

THORA THACKER

No one?

EDDIE

You're it.

*Eddie treats the deal as done in hopes that that will help make it so. He smiles at her.*

What kind of name is Thora, anyway?

THORA THACKER

It's a name that nineteen million readers trust. Don't play games with them, Eddie.

*He starts to trot off, and his gesture takes in the entire studio:*

EDDIE

Nobody's playing games here.


DESK

*Attaché case on top of the desk, bank-wrapped bills stacked inside.*

*The top of the case is swung down. The two halves of the case do not quite meet: too much money inside.*

*Straining pressure.*

*Stu Schwartz arches an eye behind horn-rimmed glasses.*

STU

Is that big enough?

*Eddie strains downward as he presses the two clasps inward, until – snap! snap! – they catch.*

CAPITOL LOT

*Eddie Mannix walks through the campus opposite-ways from last time, the attaché case bulging under one arm.*

*A woman arcs in to walk with him – a tall, red-haired woman, Thora Thacker it seems, except that her dress is different. Eddie, as when ambushed earlier, fights to conceal surprise and dismay.*

WOMAN

Hello, Eddie, I'm notifying you as a courtesy before I run tomorrow's story.

EDDIE

Hello, Thessaly, I just saw – never mind, what's up? What's the story?

THESSALY THACKER

It's about Baird Whitlock.

EDDIE

There is absolutely no truth to that old story, believe me!

THESSALY THACKER

Old?

EDDIE

Old! Stale! Rotten! And –

THESSALY THACKER

I'm talking about today.

EDDIE

And there's – (*Quick shift from heated to cagey.*) What?

THESSALY THACKER

A little bird told me he disappeared from the set today.

EDDIE

Oh! That. No no. Yes, he did have to take a break. Minor injury, high ankle sprain.

THESSALY THACKER

What did you think I meant?

EDDIE

No, nothing. I saw your sister earlier, she was trying to resurrect some old gossip about Baird.

THESSALY THACKER

I'm sure she was. That cow. She couldn't find a new story if it were taped to her posterior.

EDDIE

Well, she's –

THESSALY THACKER

High ankle sprain? That's the best you could come up with? We all know about the drinking jags and the womanizing and the trips to San Bernardino.

EDDIE

Baird is a good family man. He has a high ankle sprain.

YOUNG MAN'S VOICE

Mr. Mannix!

*A freckled youth in a cardigan sweater is bicycling up the walkway. As he furiously pedals, a Capitol Pictures pennant snaps and flutters from a high antenna off the back fender. He skids to a halt, close.*

EDDIE

What's up, Peanut?

PEANUT

Natalie told me to find you PDQ! I know it sounds screwy but she said someone's calling from the future!

EDDIE

The – good lord! Thessaly, I have to run.

THESSALY THACKER

If you do know where Baird is, let me talk to him.

*Eddie Mannix is already hastening off.*

EDDIE

Sure – well, I'll – find out where he is, right away, Thessaly, I'm sure he'll – (*Turns with a thought.*) Say, what kind of name is Thessaly, anyway?

THESSALY THACKER

It's a name that twenty million readers trust. They want the truth, Eddie.

*On his hasty retreat:*

EDDIE
Truth, yes! We're gonna give it to'm!

*He jogs off with the bulging attaché case clamped to his side, led by Peanut on his bicycle with its fluttering pennant.*


EDDIE'S OUTER OFFICE

*Eddie strides through the outer office.*

NATALIE
On two! And Hobie Doyle is in there.

EDDIE
Right.


INNER OFFICE

*Hobie, in dinner jacket, rises from the chair facing the desk.*

HOBIE
Lo, Mr. Mannix.

*As he rushes around the desk to the phone and puts down the attaché case:*

EDDIE
Thanks for coming, Hobie, one second. Mannix here, who – Damn!

*He looks at the handset he has picked up, shakes his head, cradles it. He hits a button on the phone.*

. . . Hung up, Natalie. Tell me the second they call back.

NATALIE'S VOICE
Yes, sir.

*Eddie looks darkly down at the attaché case.*

HOBIE
'T's goin on there, Mr. Mannix, looks like you're expectin' rain.

EDDIE

Nah, it's – nothing. How's the first day on the picture?
Getting comfortable?

*Eddie is still looking at the bulging attaché case. He pushes
experimentally down on the middle of its bulge. He pops the clasps.
He redistributes the currency inside – blocked from Hobie's view by
the case itself – as Hobie talks.*

HOBIE

Oh, I guess it's goin' purt good, that Mr. Lau— er,
Laur*entz*, he's an awful good man he's helpin' me get
through it, I give him all the credit in the world, me the
new hand in the bunkhouse, they got me talkin' a lot
which takes a little gettin' use to, talkin' with the camera
lookin' at me, but heck I enjoy.

EDDIE

Good, that's fine.

HOBIE

Usually on a picture I just say 'Whitey!' Or 'Whoa, there,'
but this-here it's talkin' an't's people listenin', threw me
little at first but I think I got my leg up onner now.

*Eddie has closed the case again and does the clasps. He assesses its
shape as he talks.*

EDDIE

Well, that's fine. Laurence came in this morning to tell
me how well you're doing, he's very impressed. You just
continue to do whatever he says. He knows how to make
a quality picture.

HOBIE

Oh that is true, he will not quit on a take until it has
quality –

*The phone buzzes.*

EDDIE

Hang on, Hobie. (*Punches the intercom button.*) That them?

NATALIE'S VOICE

Sorry, sir – no, do you want Mrs. Mannix on one?

*He deflates; picks up the phone.*

EDDIE

Hi, hon . . . Oh, you know – busy . . . Uh-huh . . .
Uh-huh . . . But I thought he *asked* to play infield . . .
I see . . . Well, maybe we should make him honor that
commitment . . .

*He has reopened the case and is rearranging the money.*

Well, that's true – Of course, you're right. Okay, okay, I'll
call the coach . . . Sure. Love you too.

*He hangs up.*

HOBIE

Mr. Mannix, should I run out'n get you a bigger grip?
That'n looks a little snug.

*Eddie looks up at Hobie and focuses on him for the first time.*
*A long, appraising look.*

*Hobie returns the look, not sure what it means.*

*Finally:*

EDDIE

Hobie: there's a hundred thousand dollars in that attaché
case. Ransom money. Baird Whitlock has been kidnapped.

*Hobie stares, shocked. Eddie Mannix nods a grim confirmation.*

HOBIE

Well, this is bad. Bad for movie stars ever'where.

*Eddie's mouth forms a moue of agreement.*

And you got no idea who's mixed up in this thang?

*Eddie gives a wagging headshake.*

I would look at the extries.

EDDIE

The extras. Why?

HOBIE

Well, you just never know about an extrie. They come'n
go. Everone else, I'm on the set, I look at the guy settin'

the 5K, I think, 'Why there's old Bud, settin the 5K.'
Script girl, wrangler, same thang. Extries, that's diffurnt.
Not makin a blanket call here – there's good extries'n
bad extries. All I'm sayin: you look at an extrie, you got
no idea what he's thankin'.

*Eddie stares at Hobie, contemplating.*

*The silence is broken by the buzz of his phone. Natalie's voice
comes through:*

NATALIE'S VOICE

He's back – line one.

EDDIE

Hello! . . . Yes, I have it . . . Stage Eight? . . . Right. Just
leave it there? And when do I get Baird? . . . I'll do it right
now.

*He hangs up, looks at the case, looks at Hobie.*

Can I use your belt?

WATERFRONT BAR

*We are coming off the lettering on the side of a boat which identifies
it as 'The Swingin' Dinghy.'*

*Our move reveals that behind the boat which is suspended by two
chains like a lifeboat is a backbar in the middle of which is a clock,
just now striking twelve. We move down off the clock to find a
bartender looking up at it. A dishrag is draped over his shoulder,
a well-chewed cigar stub is planted in his mouth.*

BARTENDER

The Swingin' Dinghy is closin', folks. Time for me to
clean up, time for you to clear out.

*He moves to get a broom. On his move we widen out to show the
bar's clientele: about a dozen sailors and their dates, five or six
young women. The boat of which this establishment is namesake is
a quarter-size model hanging over the bar.*

*The girls are mounting the stairs to leave the cellar bar. One turns
back with a farewell:*

GIRL

So long, fellas! See ya in eight months!

BARTENDER

Eight months?

*He is addressing a sailor whose glum look stays on the exiting girls. The look lingers on the door after it closes behind them. The sailor sighs.*

SAILOR

Yeah – we're shippin' outna mawnin.

*Another sailor, seated on the stool of a piano near the stairs, is also glum.*

SAILOR 2

Golly: eight months without a dame.

*The lead sailor, equally downcast, is played by Burt Gurney.*

BURT

Can ya beat it.

BARTENDER
(*gruff*)

You're gonna *have* to beat it.

*Visible through a high window-well which gives onto the sidewalk are the gams of a girl who has stopped to adjust the seam of one stocking.*

*Burt, gazing yearningly up at the legs, starts to sing.*

BURT

Oh, we're headin' out to sea . . .

*The production number 'No Dames!' begins.*

CORNER OF THE SOUNDSTAGE

*The song has developed and the dance begun, but here, off the set, the blaring playback is echoing and not as loud. Eddie Mannix enters the stage. He is dimly lit only by spill from the bar set, house lights turned off for shooting.*

*Eddie gives cautious looks around as he hoists the attaché case, now secured around its middle by a shiny black belt. He gingerly stows the attaché case behind an electrical box bearing the warning,* DANGER! HIGH VOLTAGE.

BACK TO THE SET

*The song finishes with Burt being ass-bounced and the bartender bellowing:*

> BARTENDER
> Now cut that out! This ain't that kind of place!

*The general pandemonium of the dancing sailors is arrested by a voice through a megaphone:*

> VOICE
> And . . . cut! Yah, okay. Okay.

*We cut behind the director seated on a canvas chair onto the back of which his name is stitched: 'Ärne Seslum.'*

> Come here, Burt Gurney. We go again.

> ASSISTANT DIRECTOR
> All right, kids, back to one!

*Burt Gurney walks up, boyishly cheerful, and is joined by the Bartender.*

> BURT
> Anything different, Mr. Seslum?

> ÄRNE
> Yah yah yah, no no no, mostly pretty good. But this time, don't put dishrag on bartender's head. You're the star of the picture, Burt Gurney. Who cares about the bartender, *you* are the star.

*The Bartender grumbles, walking away:*

> BARTENDER
> That's my whole character, the slow burn.

> BURT
> (*genuine*)
> Gosh, Mr. Seslum, I don't mind, if he wants me to –

ÄRNE

It is decided!

*Eddie Mannix walks up.*

EDDIE

Lo, Burt.

*Brightly, before heading back to the set:*

BURT

Hello, Mr. Mannix!

EDDIE

Ärne, I don't want to stick my nose in other people's business, but, uh, I understand you've been, uh, associating with DeeAnna Moran?

ÄRNE

Yah yah, we associated.

EDDIE

Yes, and she's –

ÄRNE

But no more. No more. Don't you worry, Eddie Mannix.

EDDIE

But Ärne, you are aware that she's, uh –

ÄRNE

This must not be in movie magazines, that we associated.

EDDIE

No, of course not –

ÄRNE

My wife cannot read this.

EDDIE

Your – excuse me?

*Ärne fishes out a wallet.*

ÄRNE

Ilsa Pflug.

EDDIE

Ilsa . . .?

*Ärne shows him a picture of himself and a plump woman with braids.*

ÄRNE

Ilsa Pflug-Seslum. In Malmö.

EDDIE

I was not aware of that.

*Ärne flips through, showing more pictures: himself skiing; the family posed together in cable sweaters.*

ÄRNE

Yah, yah, two children.

EDDIE
(*sotto*)

Third on the way, apparently.

ÄRNE

Do you have physical culture, Eddie Mannix? Do you ski?

EDDIE

No, I, uh, never took it up. Seems like a lot of fun.

ÄRNE

Yah, fresh air. (*Thumps himself on chest.*) Air in – (*He sucks in.*) Out – (*He blows out.*) Lungs. Breathe. (*Takes back the wallet.*) I no more associate with DeeAnna Moran – it is decided!

EDDIE

Uh-huh –

*Something on the set, past Eddie's shoulder, draws Ärne's furious look.*

ÄRNE

NO, no, no, don't swing your arms like hairy ape! This is not fat stupid people, this is Ärne Seslum production!

*Raucous male laughter hits the cut. The men are emerging from the hall into the main room, Baird and Herman in the lead, Baird's arm draped companionably over Herman's shoulder.*

> BAIRD
>
> So I feel someone poking me and I wake up and it's Clark and he says, 'Well, her keys weren't in there so I guess we're walkin'!'

*Roaring laughter from the Communists.*

> This was back before Gable was Gable.

*The men make themselves comfortable in the living room with its view of the crashing surf. It is now late day; a red sun hangs beyond the jagged rocks at the mouth of the cove.*

*Baird is lost in misty reminiscence:*

> BAIRD
>
> We used to go to San Berdoo every weekend, Bob Stack would come sometimes, the Blue Grotto was still open – Dave Chasen was a busboy . . . (*The dramatic view finally registers.*) Quite a place! Yours?

> HERMAN
>
> Oh, gracious no. It belongs to a member of our study group. He couldn't be here this afternoon – he'll be sad to have missed you. He's a fan.

> BAIRD
>
> Uh-huh, that's swell. So I black out, wake up here and I'm thinking, Baird, you have got to stop doing this! (*Laughter.*) But you're saying, actually, technically I've been . . . kidnapped.

*Again, agreeable laughter from the Communists. Herman smiles as well.*

> HERMAN
>
> Well, technically, yes.

> BAIRD
>
> And there's gonna be a ransom.

BENEDICT

I'd hardly call it 'ransom.'

*Herman indicates the speaker.*

HERMAN

Benedict there – that's Benedict de Bonaventure – wrote *The House of Ahasuaris*.

*A low whistle from Baird. Herman nods.*

Yes. Enormous hit, made the studio millions of dollars. Did you see any of those millions of dollars, Ben?

BENEDICT

I did not.

HERMAN

Dutch over there – Dutch Zweistrong – wrote *All the Way to Uruguay*.

DUTCH
(*testy*)

I wrote *all* the *All the Way* pictures.

HERMAN

All successful. You see any of the profits, Dutch?

*Dutch gives a short barking laugh.*

All of us here are writers. The pictures originated with us, they're our ideas, but they're owned by the studio. I'm not saying only writers are being exploited – I mean, look at yourself, Baird.

BAIRD

Oh, you know – the studio takes care of me.

ANGRY MAN

What're you, a child?

HERMAN
(*apology for the bad manners*)

I think what Herschel's trying to say is, just because the studio owns the means of production, why should it be able to take the money – our money, the value created by

69

our labor – and dole out what it pleases? That's not right.
So – no. No, I wouldn't call it 'ransom.'

DUTCH

Payback.

FOURTH MAN

Partial payback.

HERMAN

Now, until quite recently our study group had a narrow
focus. We concentrated on getting Communist content
into motion pictures – always in a sub rosa way, of course.
And we've been pretty darn successful. You remember, in
*Kerner's Corner* – the Town Hall scene, where the aldermen
overturn the rotten election and make Gus the mayor?

BAIRD
(*getting it, nodding*)

Oh! Yeah. Uh-huh.

HERMAN

I like to think we've changed a few minds. But then –
well, Dr. Marcuse came down from Stanford, joined the
study group. And started teaching us about direct action.
Praxis. Action.

*Faintly gesturing with his pipe:*

MARCUSE

We each pursue our own economic interest – we ourselves
are not above the laws of history. But in pursuing our
interest with wigor, we accelerate the dialectic, and hasten
the end of history and the creation of the New Man.

ANGRY MAN

Plus, we make a little dough.

HERMAN

Shut up! We're not even *talking* about money; we're
talking about *economics*!

BAIRD

Uh-huh. Sure. Good. Good stuff. So – do I get a share
of the ransom?

70

*Chuckles all around. Herman gives a weak smile.*

> HERMAN
> Well – no, Mr. Whitlock. You could hardly share in your
> own ransom. That would be unethical.

> BAIRD
> Well, I don't know if that's fair, fellas! The whole set-up
> only works if I play along, right, if I don't let on I know
> who kidnapped me?

> HERMAN
> Yes. That's right.

> BAIRD
> So what if I don't play along? What if I named names?

*The smiling faces around him harden.*

*Baird, committed, plows on:*

> . . . Just . . . told the truth?

*The alienation is palpable. Herman alone seems unruffled:*

> HERMAN
> I don't think you'll do that, Mr. Whitlock. What if *we* told
> the truth, about – *On Wings as Eagles*?

*Baird instantly sobers.*

*He looks up at the men around him, their faces set. He looks at
Herman, the only person still smiling.*


SID SIEGELSTEIN'S OFFICE

*Eddie Mannix arrives to lean against his door jamb. The legal
bullpen, rows of desks, is at his back.*

> EDDIE
> Sid, we have to work something out for DeeAnna Moran.

*Sid looks up from paperwork.*

> SID
> She get married again?

EDDIE

No, that's the problem. Having a child, *not* married.

*A whistle from Sid.*

SID

Tough.

EDDIE

Yeah. No father. Well, of course there is one, somewhere . . .

*He waves airily. Sid nods understanding.*

SID

But who knows . . .

EDDIE

Exactly. So is there any way she – I'm just spitballing here – any way she could adopt her *own* child?

*Sid gazes at Eddie. His look drifts off.*

SID

Interesting . . . As a single –

EDDIE

Mm, she disappears for a while, reappears –

SID

Uh-huh.

EDDIE

– and she wants to share her blessings – adopt a child.

SID

Sure, she's always yearned to be a mother . . .

EDDIE

That's it.

SID

Well, I don't see why not. Nothing in California statute prohibits adoption by one's own parent.

EDDIE

Uh-huh.

SID

This is new ground here. Technically, she'd have to give
up the baby, in order to adopt it, to a third . . . party –

EDDIE

Joe Silverman.

*Natalie, with clipboard, approaches from the background.*

SID

Joe Silverman, exactly. He's the foster father for a few
days. She hands the kid to Joe, he hands it back . . . I'll
do some research. (*Taps his desktop.*) This is exciting.

NATALIE

Mr. Mannix, it's five-thirty.

CAPITOL LOT

*It is a very late day. Eddie Mannix strides through the campus with
Natalie trailing.*

NATALIE

– and asked all the assistant directors. One of them said
that an extra in the courtyard-of-Sestimus-Amydias scene
seemed jumpy.

EDDIE

All right, get Walt the name of the the extra so he can
bring him in and sweat him. Walt should tell him we
won't press charges if he tells us where Baird's been taken.

NATALIE

Check.

EDDIE

If he plays dumb – or if the A.D.'s wrong and he is dumb –
check the other extras.

NATALIE

Check. Thessaly Thacker called, said you promised her
an interview with Baird today. Check that, it was Thora
Thacker.

EDDIE

No, it was Thessaly. Tell her he was at the doctor longer
than expected, she can see him on the set bright and early
tomorrow.

NATALIE

Check. And is that last part true?

EDDIE

Let's hope so. That reminds me: I need a list of everyone
who worked on *On Wings as Eagles* who's still at the studio.

NATALIE

*On Wings as Eagles* – that's a while ago, now. Aside from
Baird and the director it won't be a long list.

EDDIE

Uh-huh, get it for me. That it?

NATALIE

One more thing: a Mr. Cuddahy called, said you know him.

EDDIE

Yeah yeah.

*They are mounting a set of steps leading to a long walkway with
doors spaced at short and regular intervals.*

NATALIE

Said it's urgent he see you one last time. Suggested same
place, seven this evening.

EDDIE

What?! Why? Never mind. (*Checks watch.*) Tell him I'll be
there.

*He bangs through a door that says:*

C.C. CALHOUN, EDITING

INSIDE

*A stout middle-aged woman is at work at a clattering upright
moviola. A cigarette plumes in one hand. The room is layered with
stale smoke.*

EDDIE

Hello, C.C.

*The woman spins in her castored chair and the chair creaks as she
tips her body back so as to aim her face at Eddie. Her thick glasses
make her eyes float hugely before her face.*

*The eyes blink.*

*Her voice is emphysemic:*

C.C.

Hello, Eddie.

EDDIE

Wanna lace up what you have on *Merrily We Dance?*

C.C.

Just working on it now. I'll slap on a little music.

*C.C. brakes the picture, rolls to a trim bin, pulls track from a pin,
flanges it on the side of the moviola and then lays it under a sound
head. She snaps down the head and rolls the movie forward.*

*Eddie leans in to look at the picture cube. Glow from the moviola
screen underlights Eddie's face.*

*A fanfare. On the screen, a card:*

LAURENCE LAURENTZ PRESENTS

*Grease-marks on the print form a V that indicates a fade down.*

*As waltz music comes up, an inverted V grease-mark indicates a
fade up on a shot of the dancing feet of many couples, gowns
swirling, tuxedoed legs debonairly stepping.*

*Supered on the shot:*

MERRILY WE DANCE!

*Another fade-down mark.*

*Lateral track on the feet of a man and a woman, crossing a city
sidewalk. The man's feet hurry out of frame as we hear him call
'Taxi!'*

*The woman's feet continue on to bring into frame, when she reaches
the curb, the bottom of a cab door being opened for her by the man.*

*As she climbs into the cab we match cut into:*

*The back of the cab. The pretty young woman slides over so that a caddish young man can sit in as well. The cab starts into motion.*

> CAD

Back to your place?

> ALLEGRA

Oh, what a bore. I rather thought we might go to Lake Onondega for the weekend, just the two of us.

> CAD

Don't have my valise – I left it in your foyer.

> ALLEGRA
> (*sly*)

You'll get by without a change.

> CAD
> (*wolf*)

Suits me. If you don't mind skipping out on your own party, Allegra.

> ALLEGRA

Suits me.

> CAD

And skipping out on Monty.

> ALLEGRA
> (*smile*)

That suits me as well.

*The man laughs.*

> CAD

Poor Monty.

> ALLEGRA

What Monty doesn't know . . .

> CAD

. . . won't hurt Monty.

SWELL APARTMENT INTERIOR

*Lateral track on a pair of feet: a man walking down a hallway. As he enters a foyer he comes up short, feet turned halfway toward a valise that has been left under a table. After a considering beat he proceeds on, and we pan his feet to a door which he opens.*

*A match cut around the other side of the door onto the person entering, who is revealed to be – Hobie Doyle. We are now in the scene we saw being shot.*

> DIERDRE
> Oh Monty! Come join me on the divaaaaa . . .

*As Dierdre beckons Monty her motion slows, and her slowing speech becomes basso before lapsing to quiet and the ratcheting noise of the machine also falls quiet and we are looking at a frozen frame that slowly discolors at the center.*

*The discoloration starts to spread outward as the frame burns.*

*Eddie looks quizzically at the stalled picture.*

*A rasping voice:*

> C.C.
> Reversh.

*Eddie looks and reacts with a modest but definite take at:*

*C.C. bent double in her chair, the side of her face pressed snugly to the moviola near the gearing for the sound. The side of her face is squashed flat against the machine and something cinches the folds of fat at her neck. She is being strangled.*

> C.C.
> Reversh!

*Eddie looks helplessly at the machine.*

> C.C.
> *Reversh!*

*Eddie casts frantically about, locates the forward/reverse switch, flips it.*

*The soundtrack grinds into motion, in reverse. The picture plays likewise.*

*As the sound relays feed out her scarf, C.C. has increasing play such that she may slowly draw her head away from the machine.*

*When she is completely free she hits the handbrake, stopping the film.*

> C.C.
> Shouldn't wear scarves.

*She sucks greedily at a cigarette. She flips the reverse switch and the film rolls forward again.*

*Hobie once again enters, looking dashing in his tux.*

> DIERDRE
> Oh Monty! Come join me on the divan.

*The discolored frame flashes by and Monty sits into a brooding close shot on the divan.*

> DIERDRE
> It seems Allegra's a no-show, which is simply a bore, but I can partner you in bridge. (*Reacting to him.*) Why the pout?

*A hold on Hobie as he frames a haunted answer.*

*Finally:*

> HOBIE
> It's . . . complicated.

IMPERIAL GARDENS

*A gong stings the cut to pushing in to Arthur Fung as he gives a short bow.*

> ARTHUR FUNG
> How pleasant to see you again, Mr. Manni—

*SPLASH! A push through the curtain of beads to see Mr. Cuddahy, looking up from his booth, a drink with an umbrella in front of him.*

> CUDDAHY
> Thanks for coming back, Mannix.

EDDIE

Sure.

CUDDAHY
(*chuckling*)
You're taking us down to the wire, aren't ya?

EDDIE
It's not a ploy – just a big decision.

CUDDAHY
Absolutely! No foul. But the board was concerned when
I couldn't give 'em a yes this afternoon, and they've
authorized me to say this. You sign on, your term of
contract is ten years.

*Eddie gives a low whistle. Cuddahy nods.*

Yeah. You get it, right? That means your stock options are
guaranteed to vest. You'd never have to work again if you
chose to retire after your term. Think about it: lifetime
employment; you wouldn't be a glorified working stiff
like you are now. And you'll be running a business, not
a circus. Drink? (*Notices Eddie's look.*) Cigarette?

*Cuddahy proffers the pack which Eddie has been eyeing. Eddie
hesitates, shakes his head.*

EDDIE
No, no I – I have to run, I, I should talk this over with my
wife –

CUDDAHY
Course you should. Talk it over, think about your family,
let us know in the morning. Oh! (*Grinning, produces two
packages.*) Now, if you think this is a bribe, you're
absolutely right. Two kids, right, boy and a girl? They love
this stuff. Used to be trains.


A SPANISH-STYLE HOME

*Glowing in the early evening.*

*Reverse on its drive. Hobie Doyle leans against a parked limo with his arms folded, waiting, gazing at the mansion. A long, still beat, and then he abruptly sflflfffs sunflower shells out of his mouth.*

*He gazes idly around.*

*He has a thought.*

*He opens the back door of the limo and takes out a length of rope.*

*He starts twirling, creating a nice big loop. He expertly tips his wrist to make the loop spin level with the ground at a height of half a foot. He hops in and out of the loop.*

VOICE

Hello, Hobie.

*Startled, he muffs a hop-out and the rope dies against his shins.*

HOBIE

Oh, hello Carlotta.

CARLOTTA

Am I late?

*He coils the rope.*

HOBIE

Aw no, it ain't nothin'. Thanks an awful bunch for goin' to this picture with me, I don't know if you like livestock but I think it's got moments I really do. You look var purty.

CARLOTTA

Well, thank you, Hobie. I'm sure I'll like the picture – I like all of your pictures.

HOBIE

Well, I like yours too, they are just the craziest things. Is it hard to dance with all them bananas on your head?

*She plants her purse on her head as she demonstrates a rhumba move:*

CARLOTTA

Oh no, anyone can do it, is all inna-hips anna-lips anna-eyes anna-thighs!

*She finishes with a kick and a head-tip that launches the purse*
*backwards off her head to be grabbed by one hand behind her back.*

MANNIX KIDS' BEDROOM

*We hear a door opening and hallway light fans onto an adorable*
*little girl asleep in bed.*

*Eddie looks down at her, smiles, stoops to adjust the doll she holds*
*against her face. He rises to gaze down for another beat, then*
*moves.*

*The opposite bed: an adorable little boy. Eddie eases the askew*
*coonskin cap off of the boy, stands looking down.*

*Top of the boy's wardrobe. Baseball pennants are on the wall behind*
*it. Eddie's hands enter to place a soaring airplane on a peg on a*
*pedestal.*

*Top of the girl's wardrobe. Dolls are seated on it leaning against the*
*wall. Eddie's hands enter to place a folded maroon uniform, and, on*
*top of the uniform, a maroon cap with 'Stewardess' stitched in gold.*

MANNIX KITCHEN

*Eddie is at a plateful of dinner. His wife bustles as he eats.*

> MRS. MANNIX
> Little Eddie wanted me to tell you about his baseball
> game. They won.

> EDDIE
> That's terrific. Gosh, I never called the coach! Eddie
> played at shortstop?

> MRS. MANNIX
> Mm, and he did so well he wants to stay there now.

> EDDIE
> Great, it took care of itself.

> MRS. MANNIX
> And Darlene did very well on her Spanish test.

EDDIE

That's good, she was worried about that. Thanks for
heating up the roast.

MRS. MANNIX

Warm glass of milk?

EDDIE

No, thanks hon – coffee. Gotta run back to the studio,
a few things to take care of.

MRS. MANNIX

Gee, another late night.

*Eddie is ruminative:*

EDDIE

Mm. You know . . . Lockheed improved their offer.
Darned good money. And the hours wouldn't be crazy
like this, either.

MRS. MANNIX

It's nice to be wanted.

EDDIE

Yeah, sure, but – what do you think? They wanna know
tomorrow.

MRS. MANNIX

I like the shorter hours. But what do you think, honey?
You know best.

*Nodding, chewing, thinking:*

EDDIE

Uh-huh . . .

MRS. MANNIX

How's it going with the smoking, dear?

*Eddie is startled out of his ruminations:*

EDDIE

Oh, you know . . .

EDDIE IN HIS PACKARD

*He drives, squinting against oncoming headlights.*

*The plummy-voiced narrator:*

> VOICE-OVER
> The denizens of the great city make ready for nightlife –
> or for sleep. But Eddie Mannix will have neither . . .

BEACH HOUSE – NIGHT

*Familiar shot from high on the bluff down on the octahedral house,
now glowing with internal light. The ocean is no more than
glittering highlights caught from the moon.*

> VOICE-OVER
> Even in westerly Malibu the sun has moved on, leaving
> the vast and tireless sea to heave itself blindly upon the
> shore.

INSIDE

*We are in the living room which, it being night, offers no more view.
The writers sit playing at cards, smoking, seeking to make time pass.*

*A man circles the table dropping a pair of gloves next to each card
player – fingerless gloves with leather grips, as for golfing. The card
players little notice the deposit of gloves at their places.*

> VOICE-OVER
> Baird Whitlock has become an acolyte of the Communists,
> a convert to their cause, his belief compelled but not
> grudging – no more than was Saul's on the dusty road of
> long ago. He now seeks to learn more from the leader
> from the north . . .

*Baird is indeed sitting with Professor Marcuse, who is just finishing
talking as their conversation mixes up, with Baird nodding vigorous
concurrence.*

> . . . and becomes ever more committed to the quest to
> hasten an end to history and bring on – the New Man!

Herb – Herb! – That's exactly what I was talking about,
that's what happened when I went to Reno with Danny
Kaye and he asked me to shave his back! Exact same
thing! Because I'm thinking – who benefits? Also, I gotta
tell ya, everyone thinks Danny is a jerk but he's not really
a jerk, it's just the theory generating its own anti-theory.

*Professor Marcuse's brow furrows as he tries to follow Baird's point.*

. . . So there we are, me and Danny, and I'm wondering
what the hell I'm doing with this razor and he says it's for
a part in a Norman Taurog picture but Judy Canova is
there and she knows Norman and she says Danny's not
doing a Norman Taurog picture – he just wants you to
shave his back! And that's who benefits!


A LOBBY CARD

*It is for* Lazy Ol' Moon, *starring Hobie Doyle. When it is wiped by
a foreground cross we cut wider:*

*The near-empty lobby of a grand theater. A latecoming gentleman
and his wife are opening the auditorium door to enter, the movie's
soundtrack fanning up as they do so.*

VOICE-OVER
In livelier precincts, the swells of Dreamland gather to
inspect the complicated weave of another piece of
gossamer . . .


INSIDE

*Hobie and Carlotta are watching the movie.*

VOICE-OVER
. . . Another movie, another portion of balm for the ache
of a toiling mankind.

*Hobie leans in to Carlotta.*

HOBIE
Don't know 'bout this part, they only gimme one shot at
the song.

*It is evening. A pretty young woman converses through a cookhouse window with a grizzled old man in the yard. The man – Curly – wears the union suit and the bent-back hatbrim of a Western sidekick.*

*Someone offscreen is lazily chording a guitar.*

> CURLY
> It wasn't my fault you saw me take the pie off the sill, Miz McGraw.

> WOMAN
> Not your fault! Whose fault was it, Curly?

> CURLY
> Why, that crazy full moon! Two weeks ago you'd a never seen me take it!

*Laughter from the audience as Curly stomps over to the man playing guitar: Hobie, relaxing on a tipped-back chair on the bunkhouse porch.*

> CURLY
> Durn that moon! What good is she anyhow! Wish there never was no moon! Wish there warn't no bossy old women!

> HOBIE
> Don't blame that moon, Curly. She can't do nothin' *but* shine!

*The guitar intro has ended and Hobie launches into the first verse of 'Lazy Ol' Moon.' He looks up at the moon, occasionally looks back to the pretty woman in the window who listens, smiling.*

*As the verse ends we cut to Curly elsewhere in the yard, looking angrily down at something off:*

> CURLY
> Durn you! You turned Curly Strimlin over to the authorities for the last time!

*We cut over his shoulder: he is addressing a reflection of the moon in a watering trough. He now dives into the trough with hands outstretched as if to throttle the reflection.*

85

*Hobie sings on. Curly sits up in the trough sputtering and looks around, stymied and irate.*

> CURLY
>
> Durn! Whar'd she go?!

*Roaring laughter from the audience.*

DOWNTOWN LOS ANGELES

*Eddie Mannix pulls up in his Packard. It is late night; the street is deserted except for one swank parked car, a cream-colored luxury sedan, that stands out on this less-than-swank street. The car's uniformed driver leans against the hood smoking.*

INSIDE OFFICE BUILDING

*A wooden stairway. On the risers are painted the names of the building's business tenants. Eddie Mannix trudges up the stairs in fedora and trenchcoat with collar turned up.*

HALLWAY

*It is lined by doors with transom windows. Lettering on the pebbled glass of each office door identifies its occupant.*

*One office only shows light from inside:*

> JOSEPH SILVERMAN
> SURETIES/BONDS/ESCROW

*Eddie taps at the door.*

*It is opened by Sid Siegelstein, the studio lawyer. An inner-office door, standing ajar, shows Joe Silverman sitting at his desk: mid-thirties and, like his office, low-rent but neat and utterly without character.*

*DeeAnna Moran sits across from him in a cream-colored dress that matches her car outside, and a black hat and veil. She has a cigarette in one hand and with the other signs a document in multiple places as Joe, leaning across the desk, turns pages and points.*

We just got started – I've been taking DeeAnna through this.

*They are joining the two in the inner office, Sid now addressing DeeAnna.*

. . . So Joseph has done – well, just a whole lot of good work for us in the past. Whenever we've needed a witness or a third party for, I don't know – a petition of grievance or alienation of affection.

*DeeAnna sneaks looks at Joe as she signs pages.*

DEEANNA

And he's reliable?

*The man shows no resentment of the question and indeed no affect at all:*

JOE

I'm bonded, miss.

SID

Joe is the most reliable human being on the planet, in our experience. When Chubby Cregar was intoxicated and hit a pedestrian on Gower, we had his vehicle title transferred to Joe's name and Joe did six months in the LA County lock-up.

DEEANNA

But you're off the sauce now?

JOE

I never touch it, miss. It was a legal fiction.

EDDIE

That's exactly right. When the studio needs somebody who meets the legal standard of, uh – how did you put it, Sid?

SID

Personhood.

EDDIE

Yeah. Joe steps in and acts as the, uh . . . person.

                        DEEANNA
So you're a professional – person?

                          JOE
That's right, miss. And initial here, and here.

                          SID
Joe will be the foster parent until such time as you
adopt the child, which you can do as soon as Joe takes
possession of it.

                        DEEANNA
And he's reliable?

                          JOE
I'm bonded, miss.

                          SID
The release papers you're signing are not public record.
All these documents remain sealed until the year two
thousand fifteen.

*Joe takes the document and slides its last page into an embosser and
squeezes.*

                        DEEANNA
No one the wiser?

                          SID
No one the wiser. No fans, no court officials – not even a
notary public.

                         EDDIE
Joe himself is the notary.

*DeeAnna examines Joe, who is tensed, squeezing with both hands.*

                        DEEANNA
You must have strong forearms. Is it hard, squeezing like
that?

                          JOE
It's part of the job.

STUDIO GATE

*Scotty the guard leans out, tipping his cap, as Eddie's Packard pulls up.*

> SCOTTY
> Late night, Mr. Mannix?

> EDDIE
> Late night for both of us. Will you call Projection Seven and have'm lace up yesterday's dailies on *Hail, Caesar!*

> SCOTTY
> Sure thing. Yesterday's.

> EDDIE
> Yeah, thanks Scotty.


SCREENING ROOM

*Eddie Mannix sits slumped, hand cupped to forehead, light flickering onto him from the screen. Natalie sits on his far side with her clipboard, waiting for his attention.*

*Onscreen: we pull Baird Whitlock, in his Roman tribune's wardrobe, as he marches angrily up a line of parched and dusty slaves clamoring for water. Baird curses and exclaims 'Romans before slaves!' as he bats aside those waiting.*

*As he reaches the front of the line our pull back has brought into frame the man giving out water with a dipper. This man, whom we see only from behind, wears a simple robe and has perfectly arranged shoulder-length blond hair, slightly wavy.*

*Baird/Autolochus – once more exclaiming 'Romans before slaves!' – intercepts the dipper which the blond man is handing to a slave. Autolochus is about to drink himself when he takes in the countenance of the blond water-giver. Something in the man's face and manner strikes Autolochus mightily. He takes a staggering step back, in awe.*

*Close on Baird, his face displaying progressive waves of awe, puzzlement, hope, and ineffable wonder.*

*A flash frame and a slate for 'Hail, Caesar, Twenty-Seven Baker Two.'*

*Baird steps back into close shot with the dipper again, now displaying waves of puzzlement, ineffable wonder, some awe, then back to ineffable wonder.*

*We hear an offscreen 'Cut!' but before the flash frame Baird relaxes, his eyeline shifting as he calls out:*

BAIRD

Wuddya think a that one, was that, uh, enough, awe, or –

VOICE

Yeah, good, maybe a little more wonderment.

BAIRD

More, you mean more –

*From screen: 'Hail Caesar, Twenty-Seven Baker Three.'*

*Baird steps back into frame in awe.*

BAIRD

Hold it, sorry, wait a minute, lemme do it again.

*He steps forward then immediately steps back into frame in awe. A squinting bit of wonder.*

VOICE

Cut!

BAIRD

Was that, uh, I don't know. That one didn't really have a center.

VOICE

Yeah, no, it was –

*From screen: 'Hail Caesar, Twenty-Seven Baker Four.'*

*Baird steps back into frame, his face oddly blank.*

BAIRD

Hang on.

*His eyes leave the eyeline. He looks down, arranges his features in an expression of unutterable awe, and then jerks his look back up to the eyeline, expression locked in place.*

*A long hold, expression steady: unutterable awe.*

*Finally, hissing out of his locked jaw as he maintains the look:*

> BAIRD
>
> Howziss? Wuddya hink?

> VOICE
>
> Yeah, okay, cut.

*Eddie, watching. His eyes stay on the screen throughout:*

> EDDIE
>
> Go ahead, I'm listening.

*From screen: 'Hail Caesar, Twenty-Seven Baker Five.'*

> NATALIE
>
> Walt talked to the extra, right guy, no info – doesn't know where they took Baird, but described the truck they put him in.

> BAIRD
> (*from screen*)
>
> Was that, uh, was that – should I get to the wonderment faster?

> NATALIE
>
> Walt found the truck and found the guy who borrowed it from the guy who owns it and is talking to him.

*From screen: 'Hail Caesar, Twenty-Seven Baker Six.'*

*Eddie nods, still looking at the screen.*

> EDDIE
>
> Walt's a problem-solver, he's a good man. What else?

> BAIRD
> (*from screen*)
>
> Todd, you can – you just look like an imbecile mushed up against the camera, can you – Sam, Todd can step out, I'll just take an eyeline at the corner of the matte box. I'll hand the dipper back to, uh, to, uh, camera guy.

*From screen: 'Hail Caesar, Twenty-Seven Baker Seven.'*

NATALIE

PR just called in their report on the Hobie Doyle
premiere: warm reception.

BAIRD

(*from screen*)

Was that – I'm sorry, did you see that, I felt like I had
some spittle. Maybe Todd should step back in.

EDDIE

Good. Okay. (*Starts to rise, eyes still on the screen.*) Not
bad, have 'em use six. Is this six?


BROWN DERBY

*An orchestra plays 'Every Now and Then.'*

*Carlotta laughs, across a table from:*

*Hobie, hunched forward, very intent on what he is doing, his body
jiggling.*

*Wider: he has a strand of spaghetti and is doing rope tricks with it.*

HOBIE

Watchis now . . . Gittin' away . . .

*He ropes a salt cellar.*

Oh looka there now!

*His other hand, on the tabletop, is starting to walk away on two
fingers, affecting nonchalance.*

*Thinking itself safely out of range the walking hand starts to walk
faster.*

. . . Oh, she's a-gittin' away too!

*He ropes the walking fingers, tripping his hand.*

*Carlotta, unable to talk from laughter, points at Hobie. Hobie ropes
the pointing finger, draws her hand toward him. She slaps at his
hand with her free hand. He drops the spaghetti to slap her hand in
return and then plucks the whipping spaghetti-end out of the air in
rhythm.*

HOBIE

This's why I never order it with meat sauce.

CARLOTTA

How'd you get into pictures, Hobie?

HOBIE

Got roped into it! Aw, I'm just kiddin' ya, I wrangled fer
a while and then they saw I could say a line'r two'n I was
Bad Clem or Deppity Number Two or the guy's buddy
fer a coupla years'n then some'n heard me sing'n they
made me the guy.

CARLOTTA

You're awfully cute.

HOBIE

Aw heck, you ain't seen the half of it, I'll show ya cute,
just second here – little souvenir from when I was
rodeoin'. . .

*He has lowered his head to his hand and he fiddles briefly at his
mouth. He raises his head again, beaming at Carlotta.*

*He has no teeth. His gums, upper and lower, are hideously bare.*

*Carlotta is aghast – and then amused, more than ever. Hobie
chuckles as she laughs:*

HOBIE

Tell ya what, I wuzh shteer-bushtin an I went down and
the shteer went up'n m'teeth headed off fer easht Texash –
Aww here, it's comin round again!

*He hastily tucks his teeth back in and croons along with the
orchestra which is just now arriving at the chorus:*

Every now and then . . .

*Carlotta comes in on top:*

CARLOTTA

Every now and then . . .

*The two sing together but Hobie suddenly freezes, seeing something.*

*Long-lens point of view: a bulging attaché case bound around the middle by a shiny black belt. It rests beside a semi-circular booth, half the throw of the restaurant away. Whoever has the case is hidden by his high-backed booth. His back is to us: the side of one leg juts out as does one elbow, active as he eats.*

VOICE
Well now, this is interesting.

*Hobie's look turns up: Thessaly Thacker stands at his booth.*

THESSALY THACKER
I didn't know you two were friends.

*Hobie is distracted, his look shifting between her and the hidden man.*

HOBIE
Aw heck, yeah, we – we just caught my picture, *Lazy Ol' Moon*, 'n I guess we're –

CARLOTTA
Yes, we're friends, we're –

HOBIE
Well we're fixin' t'be friendly, tell you that.

THESSALY THACKER
That's good: 'Fixin' To Be Friendly' can be my column headline.

*Finger-quotes and an exaggerated impression of Hobie's accent set off the reference. Hobie, unoffended, nods.*

HOBIE
Well, I guess at'd be okay.

THESSALY THACKER
Have a good evening.

*As she moves off Hobie and Carlotta exchange a look: how'd we do? But Hobie's look keeps returning to the mystery diner.*

HOBIE
I mentioned the name of m'picture, I think we're s'posed to do that.

*His long-lens point of view: Thessaly Thacker has stopped to talk to the hidden man with the attaché case. Brief conversation. Thessaly tips her head back laughing at some pleasantry. Her cackle carries across the room.*

VOICE

Well now, this is interesting.

*Hobie's look turns up: it is – impossibly – Thessaly Thacker again. Or, no it isn't, it's Thora.*

THORA THACKER

I thought I was getting an exclusive on this.

HOBIE

What's that now, ma'am?

*She is looking off at her cackling sister.*

THORA THACKER

I'd like to know what the hell is going on here.

HOBIE

We, uhh . . . like I said, we just saw *Lazy Ol' Moon* –

CARLOTTA

And Hobie and I are fixin' t'be friendly!

*Thora's baleful look swings onto her. It holds for a long moment. Then a squint:*

THORA THACKER

*What?*

HOBIE

We're just, uh . . .

*His eyes widen: the mystery man is getting up. The man stands briefly outside the booth but is turned mostly away from us, patting at his mouth with a napkin. He angles more toward us.*

*It is Burt Gurney.*

*He finishes patting his mouth, tosses the napkin onto the table. His face, so boyish when performing, is now a hard mask.*

*He stoops to pick up the attaché case. A brief look around the restaurant, and he heads off.*

*Hobie hastily shuffles himself out of his booth:*

                         HOBIE
Ah gotta skedaddle. So sorry! (*To Carlotta.*) Have to catch
one a yer pictures next time – lookin' ford to it!


BROWN DERBY EXTERIOR

*Hobie exits the club just in time to see the passing-by vehicle of Burt
Gurney.*

*Hobie hurries to his car and driver waiting curbside.*

                         HOBIE
Toss me them keys, pard – I'm takin' the car!


EDDIE'S OFFICE

*Wide on Eddie behind his desk, half-in, half-out of a pool of
desktop lamplight. He sits hunched, forearms on knees.*

*An insert: on the desk is a letter, its copy too small to read. But we
see its letterhead: Lockheed.*

*Back to Eddie, but our angle now swung around so that the desk
does not hide his lower body.*

*The hands draped across his knees hold a rosary.*


BLEARY MONTAGE: HOBIE'S CAR

*Lots of neon: The Garden of Allah, restaurants, clubs, chase lights
around movie-theater marquees. Dissolving in and out under the
Hollywood Boulevard imagery is the same set-up of Hobie driving,
squinting, eyes fixed on tail lights in front of him.*

*Also dissolving in and out:*


EDDIE MANNIX WALKING

*Not his purposeful daytime stride but a contemplative stroll, hands
clasped Churchillianly behind his back. He passes through the half-
struck columns of the temple of the money-lenders; through the
courtyard of Sestimus Amydias, its fountain now giving only spare,*

*echoing drips; and finally through a set we have not yet seen: the road to Calvary, its long line of crucifixes looming empty.*

*The montage which connects the two men ends with a dissolve full up on Hobie, still driving, but with no more city lights reflected in his windshield. We are out, remote.*

*His point-of-view: tail lights of the car well ahead – the only car in sight. Its headlights briefly show us the 'Rudy's Fish Shack' sign on the right. The car turns left.*

*Hobie slows as he approaches the turn.*

HIGH FROM BLUFF

*The octahedral house glows below. Burt's car is parked. Hobie's car eases up.*

INSIDE

*For the first time the house has no interior noise, no yapping dog. We hear only the muffled pounding of surf.*

*The front door clicks, and creaks open.*

*Hobie enters cautiously, looking around at the quiet as he walks toward the lens to stop in close shot, gaping now, surprised at what he sees.*

*Reverse on the living room. Baird Whitlock is alone, a small figure in the big room, still in Roman wardrobe, a copy of* Soviet Life *open on his lap, martini glass in hand. He gapes at Hobie in mirroring surprise.*

*Finally:*

> BAIRD
> Hobie *Doyle?* You're a Communist too?

*Hobie looks around, looks back at Baird.*

*A beat.*

> HOBIE
> So it's Commies.

BAIRD

Y'ever been in this place? Pretty nice, huh? Just found out it's Burt Gurney's!

*Hobie is not really interested. He looks around a bit more, trying to make sense of it all.*

HOBIE

You here alone?

BAIRD

Everyone else went down to the beach.

HOBIE

Well, all right, pard: let's us head on back to town. You got Mr. Mannix worried sick.


PACIFIC OCEAN – NIGHT

*The Communist writers man both sides of a longboat, gloves on, pulling hard at the oars.*

*Burt Gurney stands in the prow gazing forward, rather like Washington crossing the Delaware but with a yapping dog in the crook of one arm.*

*Now his look turns to one side.*

*His point-of-view: his beach house is coming into view from behind one of a pair of jagged rocks between us and shore.*

BURT

Easy . . .

*The writers row more slowly as the house centers up between the rocks.*

Here!

*The writers back-paddle to stop the boat. It settles so as to show the house perfectly centered between the two snaggle-rocks.*

*Satisfied with the boat's position, Burt Gurney looks about: the vast and empty sea.*

*He looks at his watch: midnight.*

*A writer occasionally dips an oar for a short front- or back-stroke, keeping the boat in position. The boat dips and bobs, water slapping on wood. An occasional yap from the dog.*

*Long beat.*

*A huge roar. Seething water. Ocean surface just by the longboat roils mightily – and is breached.*

*A huge black column rises, rises, rises from the sea.*

*The writers give voice to an awed 'Oh . . .'*

*The column stops rising.*

*The roaring of great engines, and the angry hiss of water streaming from the column, subsides to . . . near-silence. Just the gentle chug of idling engines and the faint bleep. bleep. bleep. of sonar.*

*Waves slosh feebly against the imposing black column: the conning tower of a submarine.*

*The metallic screek-screek-screek of a hatch being opened. The sound moves the dog to more yapping.*

*Burt Gurney hands the dog to one of the forward writers.*

BURT

Take care of him.

*He leaps from the longboat to the sub, grabbing brackets set in a vertical line up its side: a ladder. Before he can climb, though, writers' voices exclaim 'Tell him!' 'Give it to him!' 'Give the speech!'*

HERMAN'S VOICE

Comrade!

*Burt turns, twisting from the ladder, to look back at the longboat.*

*Herman rises in front. A ripple of motion goes through the writers behind him: something is being passed forward.*

HERMAN

Comrade: we salute you! You are going to Moscow to become Soviet Man and help forge the future! We stay behind, continuing to serve in our disguise as capitalist handmaidens.

99

*Looks around, uncertain, and gets encouraging nods from the other writers.*

But the money should go to the cause, not to the servants of the cause.

*A chorus of 'hear, hear's from the writers as he gropes for a finish.*

We – well, we. . .

*The passed-forward object arrives at the man immediately behind Herman who now gives him a nudge. He turns to take the object, and turns back holding it toward Burt.*

*It is the attaché case cinched by a black belt.*

Our modest contribution to the Comintern.

*He tosses it, and Burt, with one hand anchoring him to the ladder, one-handedly catches. He looks at the case, nodding deep appreciation for what it represents.*

*He looks up.*

                    BURT
They will be pleased.

*The dog, whining and writhing in discontent in the arms of the writer in charge of him, finally breaks free and leaps yapping toward his master.*

*Burt reflexively drops the case to grab the arriving dog.*

*The case hits the water and dipsy-doodles down, down, down into murkiness.*

*The writers give a unison dismayed 'Oh . . .'*

*Burt Gurney, angled out from the ladder, gazes down at the spot where the case is disappearing. A long looking beat.*

*Finally, a small arch of his eyebrow – his only comment on life's unpredictability. He swings his body back in against the sub and climbs one-handed, holding the dog.*

*A man wearing a sable cap waits at the top. When Burt arrives the waiting man hands him a sable cap. Burt puts it on and gazes down at the longboat.*

> BURT
>
> Professor! Will you join me?

*Marcuse, near the back of the boat, gestures faintly with his pipe.*

> MARCUSE
>
> No. I will work from within.

*Burt nods concession. The man behind Burt stoops to open the hatch and both men climb in.*

*On the writers, watching.*

*The roar of engines, the seething of water. The sub descends.*

*The writers fight their oars to keep the longboat steady in the bucking sea.*

*The sub disappears. The sloshes diminish. The black sea rolls on in peace restored.*

*After a quiet beat:*

> WRITER
>
> Well, it's late. And I have revisions.

HOBIE AND BAIRD

*In Hobie's car they make the right turn from the beach access road to head south on the coast highway. Hobie hums 'Lazy Ol' Moon' as he drives; Baird gazes placidly out.*

*Baird is struck by a thought. He looks at his watch, winces.*

> BAIRD
>
> Late. I am in the doghouse.

*Hobie glances at him as Baird thinks.*

> Know what, better forget my place. Drop me at the Beverly Hills Hotel – that okay?

> HOBIE
>
> Sure.

*Both men look, attention drawn by sirens: an oncoming line of police vehicles, their rooflights spinning.*

*The cars whoosh past.*

*Baird turns to track them and Hobie looks in his rear-view.*

*The vehicles skid into a left turn at the 'Fish Shack' sign.*

*Baird faces forward again.*

*A beat.*

BAIRD

Huh!

*Fade out.*

*Fade in sound: morning birds, intermittent car-bys.*

*Fade in picture:*

STUDIO GATE

*We are looking across the street at the main gate. There is little traffic at this early hour. A cab pulls up and stops curbside. Its passenger gets out.*

*The cab pulls away and we see the discharged passenger: Baird Whitlock. Still in breastplate and leather skirt, he saunters toward the walk-through by the guard shack, whistling.*

ROAD TO CALVARY

*We track laterally with an Assistant Director who, intent on a clipboard, slowly walks past a foreground crucifix, the occupant of which, facing away from us, is in frame only to the extent of his two crossed feet. The A.D., still studying his clipboard, slows to a halt just as we bring another crucifix into the foreground. Its occupant too we see only from the ankles down.*

*The A.D. now looks up from the list on his clipboard to the unseen man on the foreground crucifix.*

A.D.

Who're you?

VOICE

Todd.

*The A.D. looks down his list. He shakes his head, still unclear; he looks back up.*

> A.D.
> Do you get a hot breakfast or a box breakfast?

> VOICE
> I don't know.

*The A.D. rolls his eyes.*

> A.D.
> Are you a principal or an extra?

*Beat. Then:*

> VOICE
> I think I'm a principal.

EDDIE'S OFFICE

*Baird, in wardrobe, is in the chair in front of Eddie's desk with his legs crossed, hands clasped behind his head, relaxed, the picture of cheerfulness.*

> BAIRD
> So I'm thinkin', 'What the hell! I've woken up in strange houses before but never without a broad next to me!'

*Eddie glares.*

> EDDIE
> (*tight*)
> Uh-huh.

*Baird, oblivious, thinks he has an audience.*

> BAIRD
> These guys were pretty interesting, though. They've actually figured out the laws that dictate, well – everything, history, sociology, politics, morality. Everything. It's all in a book called *Kapital*.

> EDDIE
> That right.

BAIRD

Uh-huh. With a K. And you're not gonna believe this, but
it even explains the stuff we do here at the studio. Because
the studio is actually nothing more than an instrument of
capitalism!

EDDIE

Uh-huh.

BAIRD

So it blindly follows these laws just like any other
institution, the laws that these guys've figured out. The
studio makes pictures to serve the system, that's its
function, that's really what we're all up to, here.

EDDIE

Is it.

*Eddie rises from behind his desk and advances on Baird, who
prattles on.*

BAIRD

Yeah, we're just confirming what they call the 'status quo.'
I mean, we might tell ourselves we're 'creating' something
of artistic value, that there's some kinda spiritual
dimension to the picture business, but what it is, is this
fat cat Nick Schenk out in New York running a factory
that makes these lollypops to pacify the – WHOOF!

*Eddie has grabbed Baird by the breastplate and hauled him to his
feet. He now slaps him, forehand and backhand: Slap! Slap!*

BAIRD

What th—

*Eddie pulls him chest-to-chest and holds him there so that he may
stare straight into his eyes as the words pour out:*

EDDIE

Now you listen to me, buster: Nick Schenk and this
studio have been good to you and to everyone else who
works here. If I ever hear you badmouthing Mr. Schenk
again it'll be the last thing you say before I have you
tossed into jail for colluding in your own abduction.

But Eddie, I didn't –

*Slap! Slap!*

EDDIE

Shaddup. You're gonna go out there and you're gonna finish *Hail, Caesar!* You're gonna give that speech at the feet of the penitent thief and you're gonna believe every word you say.

*Slap! Slap!*

You're gonna do it because you're an actor and that's what you do. Just like the director does what he does, and the writer and the script girl and the guy who claps the slate. You're gonna do it because the picture has worth and you have worth if you serve the picture and you're never gonna forget that again.

BAIRD
(*blubbering*)
Okay, Eddie, I won't forget it!

*The manhandling and Eddie's harsh tone have brought Baird to tears. Eddie releases his fistful of Romanwear with a shove that sends Baird staggering backward.*

EDDIE

You're damn right you won't. Not as long as I run this dump.

*Baird nods, whimpering, as he retreats to the door.*

BAIRD

Okay, Eddie.

*Eddie reseats himself behind his desk. Baird is reaching for the doorknob but Eddie stops him with a sharp:*

EDDIE

Baird!

*Baird turns, sniveling, hand on the knob.*

*Eddie smiles, points at him, and gives a tight nod:*

Go out there and be a star!

*It heartens Baird. He wipes his eyes with some tunic-sleeve and even manages a tremulous smile and a return nod.*

EDDIE WALKING

*He walks purposefully across the lot. Natalie is deep behind trotting to catch up, arms full of a flower arrangement.*

> NATALIE
>
> Mr. Mannix!

*He turns, waits.*

> Since you're going to your car, thought you might want to take this.

> EDDIE
>
> What is it?

> NATALIE
>
> From DeeAnna Moran. Thank you, and she doesn't need to adopt her baby after all.

> EDDIE
>
> Huh?

> NATALIE
>
> She asked Joe Silverman out for dinner last night, I guess it went well, they drove to Palm Springs and were married at three this morning.

> EDDIE
>
> Huh.

> NATALIE
>
> Will you be gone long? Today's list to go through.

> EDDIE
>
> Less than an hour, personal errand. (*Down at the flowers he holds.*) Nice arrangement.

> NATALIE
>
> She charged it to the studio.

> EDDIE
>
> Right.

*He turns from her to proceed but immediately stops with a surprised
'Gah!'*

> THORA THACKER
> Just coming to see you.

> EDDIE
> Good morning. Sorry about last night, Thora – didn't
> know your sister would show up.

> THORA THACKER
> Well, that's as may be, but I certainly learned my lesson.
> Whatever you say today, Eddie Mannix, my column
> tomorrow is about – *On Wings as Eagles.*

> EDDIE
> Thora, I wouldn't do that if I were you.

*Thora smiles thinly.*

> THORA THACKER
> I'm sure you wouldn't.

> EDDIE
> No no, you don't understand. (*Looks around.*) Let's sit
> down.


SEATING AREA

*Thora and Eddie seat themselves at a curved stone bench beneath a
stone table upon which Eddie puts the flowers.*

*Behind them is a building that says* WARDROBE. *A Roman
centurion sits against its exterior wall lacing up his sandals' calf
straps. Others emerge from the building one at a time, each cinching
up the chin strap on his bristle-topped helmet or giving the bottom
of his breastplate a tug or in some other way making ready.*

> EDDIE
> I'm telling you not to run the column, Thora, for your
> own good.

*A hoot from Thora.*

THORA THACKER

I can judge my own interest. This will be the story of the
year – and it so happens the Hearst Syndicate is looking
to pick up a Hollywood column. Hearst is four million
readers. And if I get them – Thessaly doesn't.

EDDIE

And you think this'll cinch it for you.

THORA THACKER

You know it will! Baird Whitlock, your biggest star, got
his first major part – in *On Wings as Eagles* – by engaging
in sodomy with the picture's director, Laurence Laurentz.

*She wears a smug smile, awaiting protestation.*

*Eddie only nods, equably.*

EDDIE

We've all heard the story. But here's something you
haven't heard: your source is a Communist. If you print
it, it'll be dismissed as a Commie smear tactic – and
you'll be dismissed as a Commie stooge.

*Her smile starts to fade.*

Burt Gurney has left the country and the cell he was part
of has been smashed by the police. You might've thought
he was credible because he's Mr. Laurentz's current . . .
protégé, but – you don't want to be seen as Burt Gurney's
mouthpiece after this.

*Thora's look curdles.*

*A beat.*

THORA THACKER

How did you know Burt was my source?

EDDIE

Talked to Laurence late last night, put two and two
together. (*Rises, indicating flowers.*) Well, no need to send
this since I ran into you. It's by way of apology for
Thessaly horning in last night. I do value our friendship,
Thora – (*looks at watch*) – but I'm late for something
important.

CONFESSIONAL

*Light wipes onto Eddie, rosary in hand.*

> EDDIE
>
> Bless me, Father, for I have sinned.

> VOICE
>
> How long since your last confession, my son?

> EDDIE
>
> It's been, uh . . . (*Looks at watch.*) What, twenty-seven
> hours?

> VOICE
>
> It's too often, my son. You're really not that bad.

*Eddie grimly shakes his head.*

> EDDIE
>
> I don't know, Father. I snuck another cigarette. Or two.
> I didn't make it home in time for dinner. And I, uh . . .
> I struck a movie star in anger.

*A sigh from the unseen priest.*

> VOICE
>
> All right. Five Hail Marys.

> EDDIE
>
> Okay. Okay. Father. . .

*Eddie is struggling.*

> VOICE
>
> Yes, my son?

> EDDIE
>
> May I ask you something, Father?

> FATHER
>
> Of course, my son.

> EDDIE
>
> If there's something that's easy . . . is that wrong?

> VOICE
>
> Easy?

EDDIE

Easy to do, easy to – an easy job – not a bad job, it's not bad. But then there's another job, that's . . . that's not so easy. In fact it's hard. It's so hard, Father, sometimes I don't know if I can keep doing it. But it seems *right*. I don't know how to explain.

*Silence.*

*Then:*

VOICE

God wants us to do what's right.

EDDIE

Yeah . . . (*Thinking, nodding.*) Yeah, course He does.

VOICE

The inner voice that tells you it's right – it comes from God, my son.

*Eddie glances at his watch again.*

EDDIE

Yeah, got it.

VOICE

It's His way of saying that –

EDDIE
(*rising*)

Yeah yeah, I got it.


CALVARY

*Autolochus is gazing up and off-camera as we pull him through a crowd of Israelites, his face transfigured in wonderment. As he reaches the front of the crowd he sinks to his knees. The camera pulls up and away to frame him before three crucifixes on the mount.*

*Gracchus, familiar from our epic's first scene, approaches.*

GRACCHUS

Why on your knees before this Hebrew, Autolochus?

*Baird rises, turning his attention to his friend and placing a comradely hand on his shoulder.*

AUTOLOCHUS

I encountered him before, Gracchus, beside the well of
Jehosaphat. And what manner of man!

*Gracchus doesn't understand.*

GRACCHUS

He is a priest of the Israelites, despised even by the other
priests.

AUTOLOCHUS

No. On yesterday's march, punished by the dust of the
road, I sought to drink first at the well – before the slaves
in my charge, whose thirst was greater than my own.

GRACCHUS
(*uncomprehending*)
A Roman drinks before a slave.

AUTOLOCHUS

This man was giving water to all. He saw no Romans, no
slaves. He saw only men – weak men – and gave succour.
He saw suffering, which he sought to ease. He saw sin,
and gave love.

GRACCHUS

'Love,' Autolochus?

AUTOLOCHUS

He saw my own sin, and greed, and thirst, Gracchus. But
in his eyes I saw no shadow of reproach. I saw only light.
The light of God.

GRACCHUS

You mean, of the gods.

*Autolochus gravely shakes his head.*

AUTOLOCHUS

I do not, friend Gracchus. This Hebrew is son of the one
God, the God of this far-flung tribe. And why shouldn't
God's anointed appear here, among these strange people,

in this strange place? Here, Gracchus, in this sundrenched land. Why should he not take this form – the form of an ordinary man? A man bringing us not the old truths, but a new one.

*Gracchus is willing to believe, but is confused.*

GRACCHUS

A new truth?

AUTOLOCHUS

A truth beyond the truth that we can see. A truth beyond this world, a truth told not in words but in light.

*Gracchus's chin crimps as he juts his jaw, absorbing this message.*

A truth we can see if we have but . . .

*Autolochus is staring at Gracchus. His eyes slowly narrow to a squint. His jaw eases open as he stares. After a beat of fixed staring:*

. . . if we have but – but –

DIRECTOR

*Cut.* Cut. Faith. Have but faith.

BAIRD

Faith! Faith? Not, um –

DIRECTOR

No, they changed it.

BAIRD

Goddamnit. Sorry, I'll get it, don't worry.

GRACCHUS

Could I get a pat down, I'm sweatin' like a pig.

EDDIE MANNIX AND NATALIE

*They stride across the lot, Natalie following Eddie with her notepad as at the beginning of the movie.*

NATALIE

Gloria DeLamour checked herself out of Our Lady of Perpetual Rest and showed up for work in good shape.

                    EDDIE
Nn.

                    NATALIE
Still raining in Gallup, New Mexico, and the *Tucumcari!*
crew has shot all the plates we need for *Came the Rain.*

                    EDDIE
Then – just shoot the showdown in the weather and we'll
retitle it *Tucumcari Tempest. Desert Squall. Hold Back the
Storm*. . .

*He momentarily casts about.*

                  VOICE-OVER
The stories begin. The stories end.

                    EDDIE
I dunno – bounce it off the writers.

                  VOICE-OVER
So it has been.

                    NATALIE
Check. Here's today's call list.

*She hands a sheet forward. He studies it, hands it back.*

                    EDDIE
Add a call to a Mr. Cuddahy at the Lockheed
Corporation.

                    NATALIE
Long call, short?

                    EDDIE
'Thanks but no thanks' – how long was that?

                  VOICE-OVER
But the story of Eddie Mannix –

                    NATALIE
Check. Who do we call first?

                  VOICE-OVER
– will never end.

                      113

*Eddie pushes back a sleeve to look at his watch.*

EDDIE

New York first. Time to check in with Mr. Schenk.

VOICE-OVER

For his is a tale written . . . in light everlasting.

*As they head up the walk to the administration building we boom up to bring into view the skyline of the lot beyond. In the middle distance is the Capitol Pictures water tower, one word painted on its face:* BEHOLD.

*A slanting sun, hidden by clouds, sends down golden beams.*